D0454255

WORDS OF FAITH

An Easy Reference
to Theological Terms

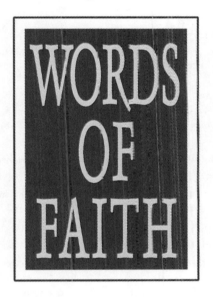

WORDS
OF
FAITH

ROB L. STAPLES

Beacon Hill Press of Kansas City
Kansas City, Missouri

Copyright 2001
by Beacon Hill Press of Kansas City

ISBN 083-411-8858

Printed in the
United States of America

Cover Design: Michael Walsh

All Scripture quotations not otherwise designated are from the *Holy Bible, New International Version*® (NIV®). Copyright © 1973, 1978, 1984 by International Bible Society. Used by permission of Zondervan Publishing House. All rights reserved.

Permission to quote from the following additional copyrighted versions of the Bible is acknowledged with appreciation:

The *New American Standard Bible*® (NASB®), © copyright The Lockman Foundation 1960, 1962, 1963, 1968, 1971, 1972, 1973, 1975, 1977, 1995.

The *New King James Version* (NKJV). Copyright © 1979, 1980, 1982 by Thomas Nelson, Inc.

The *New Revised Standard Version* (NRSV) of the Bible, copyright 1989 by the Division of Christian Education of the National Council of the Churches of Christ in the USA. Used by permission. All rights reserved.

Scripture quotations marked KJV are from the King James Version.

Library of Congress Cataloging-in-Publication Data

Staples, Rob L.
  Words of faith : an easy reference to theological terms / Rob L. Staples.
    p. cm.
  Includes bibliographical references (p.).
  ISBN 0-8341-1885-8 (pb.)
    1. Theology—Terminology. I. Title.

BR96.5 .S68 2001
230'.03—dc21   2001037910

10 9 8 7 6 5 4 3 2 1

To the many students
whose lives touched mine
during my 35 years of teaching theology
at Southern Nazarene University
and Nazarene Theological Seminary,
and whose questions forced me
to strive for clarity and simplicity
in explaining the faith

CONTENTS

Alphabetical order

FOREWORD

othing would acquaint my British visitor with American culture more quickly than baseball—or so we thought. Off we went to a major league baseball game. We took radios with earphones so my guest could hear the description of the game while he watched it. Since everyone was speaking English, we would all understand each other, right?

"A called strike?" Does that mean the players are walking out, demanding more money?

"How is a 3-and-2 pitch different from any other pitch?"

"Does a fence surround the bullpen?"

"Wilson spears a beauty in center." the radio announcer boomed. My friend looked at me: "Speared a beauty in the center?" He thought Wilson had run a spear through the abdomen of a beautiful lady. I tried to explain.

"Anderson picks up an RBI on that sacrifice fly," the announcer said.

"What's a ribey?" my friend asked, "and how do you pick it up? And who would sacrifice a fly? What is this—a religion?"

"If number 6 was thrown out by the shortstop, why is he still in the game?"

By the third inning we were both exasperated.

Church is like baseball sometimes. The insiders understand when preachers, teachers, and small-group leaders use terms like "providence" and "predestination," or "salvation" and "sanctification." But to the young and to the new people who walk into your church, it may sound like "Protestant Latin."

Baseball has been around for only a century or so, and it has communication problems. The Christian Church has had 20 times that long to drift into the use of language that's "all Greek" to the unchurched—and to more regular church members than we think.

That's where this book comes in. Rob L. Staples defines and explains 52 key terms the Church uses in special ways. These terms and the doctrines they represent spring from centuries of reflection and experience as God's people have interacted with the Scriptures, the Holy Spirit, and with life on earth. Thus, these words of faith are part of the Christian's rich heritage. They are too precious to lose, too important to neglect. They are more than mere words. They are the kinds of words the Bible says are as precious as silver and gold when spoken aptly. After all, words have "the power of life and death" (Prov. 18:21).

My former colleague at Nazarene Theological Seminary, Rob Staples, has made a career out of explaining the faith. Much of this explaining and interpreting has been in theology classes at Southern Nazarene University and Nazarene Theological Seminary. He has a gift of explaining the abstract, the theoretical, in concrete metaphors and analogies that students like me can understand.

Several years ago I invited Dr. Staples to share his gift of explanation with the readers of the *Herald of Holiness*. About half of the subjects treated in this volume first appeared in the "Words of Faith" column. The mail I received told me that readers of that column shared my enthusiasm for Dr. Staples' gift of teaching. The Evangelical Press Association acknowledged this gift in awarding its Higher Goals in Christian Journalism Award to the "Words of Faith" column. The evaluator stated, "The author has the ability to explain deep theological matters in layman's language. His biblical references are precise, his research is solid, and his issues are important."

Though Dr. Staples' theological foundation is the Wesleyan-Arminian tradition, this volume is refreshingly nonsectarian and not rigidly doctrinaire. This work is not a systematic theology, but a theological wordbook for those who do not have time or opportunity to study the heavy writings of the honored thinkers of the centuries. The aim is concise and simple (though not simplistic) explanations of key concepts of the Christian faith.

As such, this volume will be a ready resource for pastors, Sunday School teachers, small group leaders, and other church workers involved in the royal task of Christian nurture. All those who take seriously the command of Jesus to go into all the world and "teach" (Matt. 28:19-20) will find this book helpful. But it will also be an effective assistant to parents who want to teach the faith and answer the questions of their children.

Further, do not overlook the devotional qualities of this book. It can help the individual "pilgrim" pursue the holy life more insightfully. W. T. Purkiser used to say, "There can be no growth in grace until there is growth in knowledge." I think he was right. Therefore, follow Augustine's example: "Take up and read."

—Wesley D. Tracy
Former Editor, *Herald of Holiness*
(Now *Holiness Today*)

INTRODUCTION

We Christians have made a commitment (at least an implied one) to learn as much as possible about our faith and to understand the belief system the Christian tradition has handed down to us across the centuries. One way to do this is to learn the meaning of some key words that epitomize what we believe.

In the very beginning, according to Gen. 1, God created the universe simply by uttering *words*. Since we are made in God's image, the words we use can exert tremendous creative power. And since we are fallen creatures, this creative power can be turned to evil ends.

Later in Genesis, God turns the responsibility of naming things over to the people He has created. In other words, God allowed humans to be His partners in creation by the use of words. Naming things was understood as a way of bringing something into being, or at least affirming that being.

And when the author of the Gospel of John wanted to tap into this profound respect for the creative power of words, he echoed Genesis by equating Jesus Christ, who is God incarnate, with what he called "the Word."

In one sense, we humans create language. But in another sense, language creates us. The words we know and use help make us who we are. If no words existed, it would be impossible to communicate our thoughts. But then, if no words existed, it would be impossible to think thoughts in the first place. The more words we know and understand, the more thoughts we can enjoy.

Close your eyes for a moment and try thinking about something—just anything. For example, imagine you're in a boat on a lake in the midst of a storm. Such a thought would be impossible if you didn't have access to words like "boat," "lake," and "storm," or at least equivalent terms to represent the objects you've imagined. Language is one of the more important things that make us human. We would be less than human if language did not exist, although it's not necessary that our words be uttered. Even the mute person thinks thoughts that are represented by words.

In the middle of the 20th century, British writer George Orwell wrote a novel titled 1984. It was his depiction of the kind of world that could result if tendencies he saw in the societies of both East and West continued unchecked. It would be a crime to think thoughts contrary to the party line. Surrounded by "thought police" looking for "thought crime," and with "Big Brother" always watching, life would be hell on earth. One of the book's characters explained to another how Big Brother (the government) was destroying words by creating a new language called Newspeak. He said, "Do you know that Newspeak is the only language in the world whose vocabulary gets smaller every year? . . . Don't you see that the whole aim of Newspeak is to narrow the range of thought? In the end we shall make thought crime literally impossible, because there will be no words to express it. . . . every year fewer and fewer words, and the range of consciousness always a little smaller" (46).

In such a world, people would be dehumanized through their inability to express themselves. Not having words goes beyond censorship—it is the inability to think, ultimately the inability to *know*.

Fortunately, not all of Orwell's predictions came to pass by the year 1984. But the tendencies he described are still a danger in our time.

Christians dare not take lightly the importance of words for understanding, clarifying, and communicating *the* Word. They must resist all "dumbing down" attempts to limit the number, and compress the meaning, of the words used in the proclamation of "the faith that was once for all entrusted to the saints" (Jude 3).

Some words help create our Christian existence and define our Christian selfhood. This book is an attempt to clarify the meaning of some of the most important of these words. Some of these words are found in the Bible; some are not. But all of them embody biblical concepts and are significant words in the beliefs the Christian Church has passed down to us.

Reader, as you consider these words and meditate on them, make the prayer of the psalmist your own: "May the words of my mouth and the meditation of my heart be pleasing in your sight, O LORD, my Rock and my Redeemer" (Ps. 19:14).

THEOLOGY

W hat *is* theology, anyway?" The questioner was the man in the next chair who overheard me telling my barber that I had taught theology for 35 years on the college and seminary levels.

I immediately thought of the preacher who once quipped during his sermon: "Theologians are folks who give answers to the questions nobody is asking." Since the remark did not make me feel greatly blessed, I did not pass it on to my fellow haircut customer. But his question was a valid one: What *is* theology?

The word comes from two Greek words—*theos*, which is the word for "God," and *logos*, which is the word for "word." Therefore, theology means "a word about God."

To say that theology means "the word of God" would be a mistake. We call the Bible the *written* Word of God, and we call Jesus Christ the *living* Word of God. And following Augustine, we call the sacraments the *visible* Word of God.

Theology, then, is not the Word *of* God. It is a word *about* God. Thus, it is a *human* word. It is the human attempt to understand and express the truth and the grace that God imparts to us in His Son and in the Scriptures and in the sacraments. But the word *logos* could also be translated as "discourse," "study," or even "doctrine." So theology means "a discourse about God," "the doctrine of God," or "the study of God." Or, if you prefer, it simply means "God talk."

But that doesn't say it all. In theology we talk and study not only about God, but also about the creation, humanity, sin, Christ, salvation, the Church, and what we usually refer to as the "last things" (such as death, resurrection, judgment, the Second Coming, heaven, hell, and so on). We theologians use some big words for these topics. We call them, respectively, cosmology, anthropology, hamartiology, Christology, soteriology, ecclesiology, and eschatology. But don't let those words scare you. Every profession has its own jargon, and theology is no exception. But the meaning of each of those words is really quite simple.

You may ask, "If theology is the study of creation, humanity, sin, salvation, and such matters, why do we define it as the study of God?" The answer is that in theology all these subjects are studied from the standpoint of their *relation to God*.

For instance, cosmology (from *cosmos* and *logos*) means the study of the creation, or the world. But in theology we don't study the world as we would study it in geography, geology, or other scientific disciplines. We study the world as the creation of God and the object of His care. We study about God as the source and ground of the universe. So whether we're studying the world, sin, the Church, or any other topic, we look at the object being discussed in the relation it has to the Being we call God. Theology, then, can still be called "the study of God."

Well, not quite! We who work in theology don't talk much about "studying" theology. We prefer to speak about "doing" theology. Theology is not merely something you think about—it's something you *do*. A former teacher and colleague of mine, J. Kenneth Grider, liked to tell his students that "theology wears overalls." He meant that theology is not an intellectual game played on a mental chessboard in some "ivory tower" away from the real world. Theology is *life!* Our theology affects all we do. The work of theology takes place "where the rubber meets the road"—at the point where our beliefs and our everyday lives meet.

Jesus gave us a rich insight into what theology is, even as He commanded us to *do* theology: "Love the Lord your God with . . . all your mind" (Mark 12:30). Theology is loving God with the mind—all of it!

Theology deals with our belief system. Everyone believes something. We all have a "theology," whether we know it or not. It's better to know it. It's even better to try to understand the theology we have. Great medieval thinker Anselm of Canterbury spoke of theology as "faith seeking understanding." What does *your* faith seek?

See also
   Creation
   Trinity

AUTHORITY

W hy do we believe what we believe? What is the source from which we derive our religious faith? Do we say, "Nobody can tell me what to believe—I believe in whatever I decide is good for *me*"? Or do we simply (and simplistically) say, "The Bible says it. I believe it. That settles it." Both extremes are off the mark.

Although John Wesley, our spiritual and theological mentor, continually quoted Scripture, his view of biblical authority was broader than a mere proof-text approach. Students of Wesley have often discussed what they call "the Wesleyan quadrilateral." In plane geometry, a quadrilateral is any figure with four sides, such as a square, a rectangle, or a trapezoid. At different times Wesley wrote of four sources of religious authority—Scripture, tradition, reason, and experience. All were authoritative for religious belief. These four "sides" of authority were not equal, however, for Scripture was primary. The other three were merely subsidiary authorities.

Actually, Wesley invented nothing new. He simply articulated the way Christians through the ages have arrived at faith. When doctrinal reflection has been at its best, there has always been an interdialogue of Scripture with tradition, reason, and experience.

But why do we need any "subsidiary authorities" if we have the inspired Scripture? Because a person's interpretation of Scripture can easily be influenced by factors having little to do with Scripture. This can result in all kinds of bizarre ideas purporting to be biblical. That's where the subsidiary authorities offer help.

Tradition, the first of the subsidiary authorities, is what the Church has believed throughout its history, in which the accumulated wisdom of one generation is passed on to the next. Although the years have brought much variation in belief, there is also a common thread, a mainstream of teaching, that has remained constant. The triune God, the deity of Christ, the fact of sin, the necessity for atonement, for instance, have all been taught through the ages. An honest regard for Christian truth will not lightly dismiss what the Church has proclaimed through the centuries.

Reason, the God-given capacity to think, is another subsidiary authority. Of course, reason cannot be the final source of truth, for the human mind has been corrupted by sin. But God graciously continues to let reason function in significant ways, and logical consistency is not an enemy of devout faith. However one may interpret the Book of Jonah, it is not beyond God's ability to miraculously keep the prophet alive for three days in a whale belly. But if the Bible had claimed that *Jonah* swallowed a whale, our reason would rightly balk at that assertion; or when the psalmist writes that God is a "rock" (Ps. 18:31, KJV), reason tells us he is writing metaphorically, not literally. Or when Jesus describes King Herod as a "fox" (Luke 13:32), reason tells us that He's not saying Herod was actually such a four-legged creature. In such instances, and also in more complex situations, reason has a place in the structure of religious authority. Wesley said, "To renounce reason is to renounce religion. . . . Religion and reason go hand in hand, and . . . all irrational religion is false religion" (*The Letters of John Wesley*, 5:364).

Finally, *experience* is another factor in religious authority. For Wesley, the truth of Scripture needs the confirmation of experience. If what he preached from Scripture could not be authenticated in the living experience of real people, he would conclude that he had misunderstood Scripture. On the matter of entire sanctification, for example, he asserted that if he were convinced no one in England had experienced it, he would preach it no more (*The Works of John Wesley*, 11:405-6).

In reality, the final religious authority for Christians is not Scripture, tradition, reason, or experience. It is *the gospel*. But it is the gospel as faithfully recorded in *Scripture*, kept alive and passed on to us through the historic Christian *tradition*, explicated and clarified through *reason*, and authenticated in human *experience*. In reality, the Gospel (and thus our final authority in matters of faith and practice) is Jesus Christ. He is the Word of God incarnate. We believe what we believe because this Living Christ has grasped us. And what we believe we joyfully proclaim.

See also
   Scripture
   Inerrancy

SCRIPTURE

T he Bible is the manger in which Christ is laid." With that concise and graphic metaphor, Martin Luther explained his view of Scripture.

The great Protestant reformer was utilizing Luke's account of Jesus' birth, in which shepherds found the Christ child lying in a manger. The manger itself was not the shepherds' ultimate goal. They were looking for the newborn babe, and the manger was simply the place where the angels told them to look.

The point of Luther's analogy is that Christ, who is the living Word, is found in the Bible, which is the written Word. But the latter is simply an instrument directing us to the former—and thus not an end in itself.

Let me construct a story, playing off Luther's metaphor. In my story are four shepherds. After all, the Bible does not tell us how many of them came to the manger. I suppose we have three shepherds in the children's Christmas pageants in order to balance the three wise men on the other side of the stage also dressed up in their fathers' bathrobes. But the Bible is also silent on the number of wise men present. Christian art and legend have portrayed three wise men perhaps because there were three gifts—gold, frankincense, and myrrh.

So my story has four shepherds—three representing various theological viewpoints that are widespread in toda's religious climate and one representing the Wesleyan viewpoint. One by one they come to the manger (remember that the "manger" is the Bible), seeking the Christ.

The first shepherd comes to the manger and says, "This is a weak manger; some of the boards have knotholes in them." So he tries to make it better by ripping out the "miracle" boards—the "Virgin Birth" and "Resurrection" boards. Pretty soon he has weakened the manger so much that Christ falls into the straw onto the stable floor!

Then the second shepherd rushes up. "I'll defend the manger," he says. "I'll fight anyone who tinkers with it. Let no one lay a hand on it." He spends most of his energy defending the manger and practically idolizing the boards (the written words), leaving little time to adore the Christ (the living Word) who lies in it.

The third shepherd probably never even bothers to find the manger. He thinks the angel's announcement of a newborn king is a nice story, but only one story among many. It has meaning for some people. Other stories are meaningful to others, and who can say which story is most important? We can each create our own stories, and one is as true as another.

Now the Wesleyan shepherd differs from them all. Unlike the third shepherd, he knows he must go to the manger (the Bible) to learn about Christ. There are many mangers (books) in the world, but only this one has the words of eternal life. But having come to the manger, he differs from the first shepherd, who wants to reconstruct it. The Wesleyan knows that this manger is truly unique. Of all mangers (books) in the world, this is the most important. He respects it, loves it, and handles it with care. But he does not worship it. Having come to the manger, he, unlike the second shepherd, does not tarry, avoiding adoring the manger itself. He does not defend it, believing its truth is strong enough to defend itself. He quickly turns to worship and adore the Christ lying there, and then he goes and proclaims Him.

Someone might say, "Wait a minute. Haven't you slanted this story to make it come out the way you wanted?"

I answer, "Of course, it's my story. You may develop your own story and slant it as you wish." But this is my simple way of explaining the place the Bible has in Wesleyan theology.

Luther was correct in calling the Bible the "manger" in which Christ is laid. He also said, "Christ is Lord and King of Scripture." In these respects, Wesley was much like Luther. The center of the Bible is Jesus Christ. The written words are important. But they're important for one main reason—they point us to the living Word, whom alone we worship and adore.

See also
   Authority
   Inerrancy

INERRANCY

Throughout a good part of the 20th century, a fierce debate has raged among Evangelical Christians over the question of whether or not the Bible contains any errors. We in the Wesleyan tradition have avoided the divisiveness some denominations have suffered whenever the "inerrancy" issue has reared its ugly head.

Wesleyanism differs from Fundamentalism, which arose early in the 1900s and is rooted mostly in Calvinistic soil. Fundamentalism rests on a particular concept of Scripture, which may be called (pardon the use of some complicated words here) "epistemological inerrancy." Epistemology is the branch of philosophy that investigates the origin and nature of knowledge. Fundamentalism believes the basic question in theology to be *What is the source of knowledge?* Only after the source of knowledge (and thus of truth) has been established as reliable can we discuss other matters such as salvation. Since the Bible is epistemologically inerrant (that is, everything it says on any subject must be true), we can trust its message of salvation; otherwise it could not be trusted.

Harold Lindsell is an articulate spokesman for this position. He says, "Of all doctrines connected with the Christian faith, none is more important than the one that has to do with the basis of our religious knowledge. . . . The root question is: From where do I get my knowledge on which my faith is based?" (*The Battle for the Bible,* 17).

But Wesleyan theology works differently. For Wesleyanism, the basic theological question is *What must I do to be saved?* The crucial issue is salvation. "I want to know one thing," said John Wesley, "the way to heaven; how to land safe on that happy shore" (*Works,* 5:3). The Wesleyan concept of scriptural inerrancy is one of (pardon another complicated phrase) "soteriological inerrancy." Soteriology is the branch of theology that deals with salvation. In Wesleyan theology, salvation *is* truth. Truth is determined by what salvation is, not the other way around. The Bible is sufficient for salvation. It cannot fail to lead us to God and to heaven if we obey

its precepts; that is what it means to say it is inerrant. In Fundamentalism, knowledge is the foundation, and salvation is the superstructure. In Wesleyanism, the opposite is the case—salvation is the
foundation, and knowledge is the superstructure. When we know
the source and way of salvation, we know ultimate truth. This
means that truth is centered in Jesus the Christ, for He who is the
Word says, "I am the Truth" (see John 14:6).

Such a view of what I call "soteriological inerrancy" is affirmed
in the Nazarene Articles of Faith. Under the guidance of late Wesleyan-Holiness theologian H. Orton Wiley, the church wisely drew
up a statement that affirms inerrancy but avoids the Fundamentalist
version of it. It says in part, "We believe in the plenary [that is, full
or complete] inspiration of the Holy Scriptures . . . inerrantly re-
vealing the will of God concerning us in all things necessary to our
salvation."

This does not mean that we can separate the Bible's teaching
about salvation from its statements about other matters and claim
that the latter may contain errors while texts that speak of salvation do not. That would be a precarious position. Who is to decide
how to separate the two kinds of texts? Who is to say whether a
text does or does not relate to salvation? We believe that the
Bible—all of it in its wholeness—is sufficient to lead us to God and
salvation. The Bible was not written as a textbook for all branches
of knowledge. It was written to show us the way to heaven. It is
completely sufficient for that end. Wesley wrote, "God himself has
condescended to teach the way: For this very end he came down
from heaven. He hath written it down in a book. O give me that
book! At any price, give me the book of God! I have it; here is
knowledge enough for me" (*Works*, 5:3).

And for me! Some people try to make the Bible say what God
never intended it to say and then come to swords over whether it is
inerrant in saying it. Such folks may battle with each other if they
wish, but as for me, I want to know one thing—the way to heaven.

See also
    Scripture
    Authority

GOD

"I n the beginning God . . ." So begins the Bible. It offers no attempt to prove God's existence. The Bible simply starts with that assumption.

Theologians through the ages have tried to prove God's existence. But I question whether people can really be argued into believing in God. Belief is more likely to *precede* rather than *follow* an understanding of such arguments. Yet such reasonings, with varying degrees of cogency for different people, do clarify the meaning of God for the thinking mind. Though rational arguments cannot compel belief, they can clarify what is involved in believing and make a person's belief (or even unbelief) more authentic.

Still, in a sense, we are presumptuous to try to get behind the Bible's starting point and define God. God is not an object human beings can manipulate or circumscribe by their own reasoning. God is the unfathomable Mystery—

> *Immortal, invisible, God only wise,*
> *In light inaccessible hid from our eyes.*
> —Walter Chalmers Smith

Doesn't the Old Testament commandment forbidding us to make "graven images" of the deity mean we have no right to compare God with anything known to us? He is incomparable, and so He cannot be known.

And yet when we say this, we have already begun to know God! For this is precisely the knowledge of God—that God cannot be defined. Here is mystery. The more we know God, the more we experience the truth that this mystery is unknowable. We draw nearer to God when we acknowledge this.

The gods of paganism were not really mysterious. People could know them within the sphere of the natural—either in the processes of nature or by the discovery of the human mind. The mystery of the pagan gods was merely the mystery of nature, not the mystery of something authentically supernatural.

The Bible teaches us that only by revelation can we understand

the mystery as mystery. Only when we meet God in His own revelation do we fully understand how unknowable God is. There we learn
that our own processes of knowing do not bring a true knowledge of
God, since through them we remain in our human sphere. As Emil
Brunner has pointed out, He alone is mysterious who comes to us
from a sphere beyond all spheres known to us, breaking through the
barriers of our own experience of the world, and enters into our
world as one who does not belong to it (*Dogmatics*, 1:118).

That is exactly what God did! That's the meaning of the Incarnation. And there we attain the true knowledge of God.

In the past, theology teachers often made a capital error, first
examining the doctrine of God, noting definitions of deity and
then later focusing on Christology—the study of the person and
work of Christ. Then, trying to establish Christ's divinity, they
sought to show how Christ measures up to definitions of God already established. But by following that procedure, they worked
backward, for Jesus Christ reveals to us exactly what God is like.
For Christians, God is "the God and Father of our Lord Jesus
Christ" (Rom. 15:6; 2 Cor. 1:3; Eph. 1:3; 1 Pet. 1:3).

And now we know what God is like—He is like Jesus. He is the
self-giving and self-emptying One. Paul tells us that Jesus, who was
in the form of God, "did not regard equality with God as something
to be exploited, but emptied himself, taking the form of a slave"
(Phil. 2:6-7, NRSV).

So now we know! If Jesus is the perfect revelation of God, as
Christian Faith has always proclaimed, if Jesus defines God for us,
then emptying himself, giving himself away, investing himself in
others, and becoming a servant—totally and without reservation—
that is precisely what it means to be God! Such an understanding
runs counter to all definitions of God that we construct in our human ingenuity, logic, and rationality. But the understanding of God
is what His Son has revealed.

See also
   Trinity
   Mystery
   Holiness

TRINITY

To some people, the doctrine of the Trinity is a perplexing puzzle. "How can anything be both one and three?" they ask. This sounds like mathematical nonsense. Isn't it doctrinal double-talk to profess faith that "The LORD our God, the LORD is one" (Deut. 6:4) and then sing the words of Reginald Heber's hymn, "God in three Persons, blessed Trinity"?

The doctrine of the "triune God"—perhaps a better term than Trinity—was never meant to be a puzzle, although it certainly is laden with *mystery*. In the New Testament, a "mystery" (*mysterion* in Greek) is something hidden in God's eternal and inscrutable will, which cannot be discovered by human reason alone but that *has now been revealed* to believers through Jesus Christ (see Rom. 16:25-26; 1 Cor. 2:7-10; Eph. 1:9; 3:9; and Col. 1:26).

Still, we must be careful. It is not that God has revealed to us directly that the divine being is triune. Nowhere does the biblical revelation tell us explicitly that God is "three persons in one substance," as the later creeds phrased it. God never says "I am three." Most certainly God does not say "*We are* three." What is said, if we listen carefully to the scriptural revelation, is this: "I *am*," "I am *here*," "I am here *for you*." God has simply revealed Godself.

But then when Christian thought reflects on the meaning of God's self-revelation—on just how it is that God *is*, and that God is *here*, and that God is here *for us*—it arrives at the concept of the triune God. Thus, the concept of the Trinity arises out of revelation. Another way to say it is that our doctrine of God arises out of our *experience* of God.

The 12 disciples of Jesus were devout Jews. As such, they believed in the God of Deut. 6:4, the one Lord of Israel. But they had met a man named Jesus who called them to follow Him. As they followed Him, they at first had no comprehension of His deity. But after Calvary and the Resurrection, they realized that when they had been in the presence of Jesus, they had been in the presence of

God. What God? Not some second God, but precisely the *one* God of Deut. 6:4, whose glory they had seen in the face of Jesus Christ (2 Cor. 4:6).

Then after His ascension, when Jesus was no longer with them, and after the outpouring of the Holy Spirit at Pentecost, they became aware of God in yet a third way. God was living *within* them! What God? Not some third God, but the one God of Israel who is also the Father of the Lord Jesus Christ.

With that kind of experience, the early Christians began to understand the "threeness" of God, and eventually the theologians began to construct doctrines of the Trinity.

In short, God the Father is God *beyond* us—the Creator and Governor of the universe. God the Son is God *beside* us—the Redeemer who came into our world and became one of us. And God the Holy Spirit is God *within* us—the indwelling Comforter and Sanctifier.

In relation to time and space, there are only three ways God can be God. First, God is God everywhere and always—in *all* places and in *all* times. Second, God is God there and then—in *one* place and in *one* time, becoming incarnate in human flesh. And third, God is God here and now—in *my* place and in *my* time, working within me to conform me to His divine image. Those three statements say about all that needs to be said. They cannot be increased to four and cannot be reduced to two.

That is what we mean when we confess our faith in the one triune God, not three separate Gods—that would be nothing but heathen polytheism—but one God who is triune in essential being. God with three faces, as it were. Interestingly, our word "person" has come down to us from the New Testament Greek word *prosopon*, which means "face" by way of the Latin term *persona*, which means "mask."

This one God is our Creator, our Redeemer, and our Sanctifier. God in *three* persons, blessed Trinity! The Lord our God is *one* Lord!

See also
>   **Theology**
>   **Mystery**

CREATION

"D addy," asked my oldest daughter when she was four years old, "when God made the world, what did He make it out of?" Although she didn't realize it, she had asked a profound question.

There are only a few possible answers: First, God made the world out of *something*—some preexistent matter—as a sculptor carves a statue out of an existing block of marble. This image conveys the idea of purpose, bringing out the skill of the creator and allowing the order and beauty of the resulting creation to be appreciated. But it is deficient, because it portrays God as giving form to something that's already there, thus positing another eternal reality outside of God. Such a view is called *dualism* and was taught by some of the earliest Christian heretics.

Another view holds that the world was not made out of *something* but is simply an emanation from God himself. This is called *pantheism* ("God is all, and all is God"). The world simply arises out of God, as heat radiates from a fire, or light from a lamp. The strength of this image lies in the organic connection it makes—between the Creator and the creation. But its strength is also its weakness. It blurs the distinction between Creator and creation, implying an automatic or involuntary emanation rather than a conscious decision to create. The world just bubbles up out of God's being, as lava flows from a volcano.

Another view is *panentheism*, which draws a distinction between God and the world but holds that the world is "in" God, is part of God, is God's "body," as it were. The "world as God's body" analogy is that God is to the world as our mind is to our physical body. The body does not always do what the mind wants. There are varying degrees of freedom in all created things. For example, body cells may "go their own way," becoming cancerous. This view illuminates the mystery of suffering, showing God is not to blame for it. It also affirms the effectiveness of intercessory prayer. If I'm a part of the world, and the world is a part of God, when I pray a change occurs in the world and even in God! "Prayer changes things" becomes much more than a slogan. However, some find in this view an inadequate basis for conceiving of an interpersonal relationship to God, holding that in such a view God's relationship to me would be analogous to my relationship to a cell in my body, not a dialogue between *personal* beings.

Another view holds that the world was created *out of nothing* (Latin: *ex nihilo*). God brought into being something that did not exist before and that would not exist at all except for God's decision to create. This has been the predominant view throughout most of Christian history.

All these views have both strengths and weaknesses. The real purpose of the doctrine of creation, however, is not to explain how God did it or "what he made the world out of," as my young daughter put it. The doctrine of creation is more *devotional* than philosophical. When we confess, in the words of the Apostles' Creed, that God is the "Maker of heaven and earth," we make at least these significant affirmations:

1. *The world and all beings in it are totally dependent on God.* "In him we live and move and have our being" (Acts 17:28). God is not the "divine watchmaker" who made the universe, wound it up, and left it to run by its own power.

2. *The creation is essentially good.* The Creator himself passed this judgment on it at each step in the creative process (Gen. 1:10, 18, 21, 25, 31). Although the world as we now experience it is "fallen" and in need of redemption (Rom. 8:18-22), to affirm its goodness is not only to say it was good as it came from the Creator's hand, but that God's ultimate purpose for it is good.

3. *We are stewards, not owners, of God's creation* (Gen. 1:27-30). We hold it in trust for God. This has implications for the natural environment. To confess faith in God as Creator is to resist, as much as possible, the wanton destruction of natural resources and the pollution of earth's rivers, oceans, and atmosphere. All created things and people are interdependent.

Let us then confess, "I believe in God the Father Almighty, Maker of heaven and earth."

See also
   Time

PROVIDENCE

I t must have been providential." How often have you heard that assessment of some event that has taken place? When there seems to be no natural reason why something has happened, we often resort to calling it an act of providence. That's not necessarily bad—providing we understand what providence is.

The doctrine of providence is correlative (a twin, one might say) of the doctrine of Creation. The latter is an affirmation of our faith that God is the source and ground of the universe. In the doctrine of providence, we affirm our faith that God continues to sustain and govern what He has created. "In him we live and move and have our being" (Acts 17:28). "Providence" is not a biblical word, but it *is* a biblical concept prominent in the teachings of Jesus (see Matt. 5:45; 6:25-34; 10:29-31).

The idea of providence can easily be perverted and peddled like a patent medicine that will cure everything from falling hair to athlete's foot. It must not be confused with its popular counterfeit. Some people claim that Christianity will make you rich, healthy, lucky—or all three. "Become a Christian," say these purveyors of the prosperity gospel, "and you'll have everything you want." The truth is—becoming a Christian has gotten a lot of people killed! As Dietrich Bonhoeffer reminded us, when Jesus calls us to follow Him, He bids us come and *die!* Grace is the absolutely free gift of God that costs *us* everything. Salvation is free, but discipleship is costly.

Providence is not the same as the concept of absolute predestination taught in some traditions, that God determines all events or that everything that happens is God's will. It does not mean that everything that happens to the Christian is understandable or that we will always be free from trouble. It means that nothing can separate us from God, that, as the familiar spiritual puts it, "He's got the whole world in His hands."

The greatness of Christianity lies in the fact that it does not seek a supernatural *remedy* for suffering, but a supernatural *use* for it. Authentic Christian faith does not deny suffering, anxiety, despair,

or death. Rather, it proclaims that God can use it all for His purpose of love. God demonstrated this most profoundly when He
himself suffered and experienced anxiety, despair, and death in Jesus Christ. The Cross is the Christian's point of reference, the perspective from which he or she understands the providence of God.
It is never a mere theoretical proposition to be debated, but always
a personal confession to be lived.

Belief in providence is not fatalism. Fatalism is the assertion
that you "can't win," that "the dice are loaded," that "the cards are
stacked against you," that there is a cold, unchangeable, impersonal
fate that rules all things. The ancient Greeks believed that gods,
humans, and nature are all inextricably caught in the web of fate
from which there is no escape. The fatalist believes that life is, in
the words of William Shakespeare in his play *Macbeth*, "a tale told
by an idiot, full of sound and fury, signifying nothing."

Christian faith in providence is the absolute opposite of the
Greek surrender to fate. It is personal trust in a personal God, a living
faith in a living God who confronts living individuals. The apostle
Paul's understanding of providence is expressed in Rom. 8:28: "We
know that in all things God works for the good of those who love
him, who have been called according to his purpose." Paul does not
deny the existence of evil. He does not claim that all things are good,
or that all things of themselves work together for our good. Rather,
he says that *in* all things (evil, pain, suffering, loss, grief, or whatever)
God is working to bring about good for those who love Him.

This is one of the exasperating aspects of the Christian faith for
people who do not share it. Those who trust their wealth, their
health, or their stealth are utterly confounded when they meet
Christians who are willing to take whatever comes, in the knowledge that God is working in it for their ultimate good. In the face of
evil, and with God's eternal purpose in view, Christians can affirm
with Paul, "I know whom I have believed, and am convinced that
he is able to guard what I have entrusted to him for that day" (2
Tim. 1:12).

See also
   Predestination

MIRACLE

M iracle" has become a bloated word in today's vocabulary, suffering from the inflationary tendencies of our language. Sportscasters often exemplify this tendency. A wide receiver catches a difficult forward pass in a football game, scoring the winning touchdown, and the announcer excitedly proclaims it "a miracle catch." The advertising industry contributes to the inflation. There are miracle drugs, miracle fabrics, miracle detergents, miracle foods, and miracle diets.

A woman in Iowa gave birth to seven babies. The news media went wild and called it a "miracle." In a sense, all births may be miracles, but the fact there were seven of them did not make it a miracle. That statistic was the result of the mother taking fertility drugs. It must have been an overdose!

Television preachers discredit the word when they promise us miracles—especially if we'll send an offering "to keep this ministry on the air."

So what *is* a miracle? A typical dictionary definition is "an event that deviates from the known laws of nature, or transcends our knowledge of those laws." There are two problems with this: (1) It implies that nothing would be considered a miracle if no natural laws were known, and (2) It implies that nothing could be considered a miracle if *all* natural laws were known.

So we may as well stop trying to understand a miracle by considering its relation to the laws of nature. "Natural law" is a scientific concept anyway. It is not causal or determinate but simply a description of the way things in nature are generally observed to behave.

"Miracle," on the other hand, is a theological concept. Christian faith is not committed to the absoluteness of any physical law. It simply asserts that nothing in this universe, including so-called natural law, is independent of God. "In Him we live and move and have our being" (Acts 17:28).

For the believer, any event that opens one's eyes to God can be seen as a miracle. God can make any event transparent so that we can see Him revealed in it. Miracle, then, "is virtually synonymous with revelation," says H. Ray Dunning, "all genuine miracles from the biblical perspective are revelatory, and all revelation is miraculous (in contrast to merely human discovery)" (*Grace, Faith, and Holiness*, 261).

The same event that may be a miracle to the believer may not be a miracle to the unbeliever. Judas probably saw as many miracles as the other disciples, but this did not keep him from betraying Jesus. On the Day of Pentecost, that which was seen by the believers as the outpouring of the Holy Spirit promised by the prophet Joel was for those who did not want to believe merely the result of early morning drunkenness.

There is no way a skeptic can prove that real miracles don't occur. As C. S. Lewis pointed out, we can be assured that miracles do not occur only if we already know that all reports of them are false, but we can know that all reports of them are false only if we already know that miracles do not occur! Thus, the attempt to disprove miracles is a circular exercise, like a dog chasing its own tail.

Faith in the reality of miracles, however, must not lead us into a serious misunderstanding. This is the idea that events usually run without God's intervention—by themselves, so to speak—and only occasionally does God enter into the processes of nature and perform a miracle. Then, when He has finished with the miracle, He withdraws and lets things run by themselves again. This view, known as deism, makes God a spectator to the processes of nature, who only now and then takes a direct interest in these processes.

On the contrary, biblical faith declares that God in Christ is continuously "upholding all things by the word of his power" (Heb. 1:3, KJV). He is not the "divine Watchmaker" who winds up the universe and leaves it to run by its own power.

The people of the Bible did not distinguish between "natural" and "supernatural" events. Some events were just more unusual than others. But all events—the usual and the unusual—could become the occasion of faith for those with eyes to see. *That* was a miracle. It still is!

See also
   Creation

SATAN

C hristians do not believe in Satan. They believe *against* him. Such an assertion, please note, is not a denial of Satan's existence. There is an evil one, and Christians know who their enemy is. The Christian's faith in all its power is directed *against* him.

But we don't believe "in" him in the same way we believe in God the Father Almighty, in Jesus Christ, and in the Holy Spirit. Faith in that sense means trust. We dare not trust the devil! Satan is not mentioned in the Apostles' Creed, nor the Nicene Creed, nor in any of the historic creedal affirmations of the faith in which we confess what we believe "in." The very confession of our faith is a "renunciation of the devil." Yet the power against which we believe, against which faith is faith, has its own reality.

The biblical witness sees this enemy as a power. He appears in the parable of the wheat and the tares (Matt. 13:24-30) and as the biblically well-versed tempter who encounters Jesus in the desert (Matt. 4:1-11). He appears before God to test Job, and he appears before God's messenger to accuse him in Zech. 3:1-2. He is the power whose very being is the lie. "When he lies, he speaks according to his own nature" (John 8:44, NRSV). "The devil has been sinning from the beginning" (1 John 3:8) and prowls among Christians "like a roaring lion" (1 Pet. 5:8), transforming himself into "an angel of light" (2 Cor. 11:14). He is mentioned in the Lord's Prayer as "the evil one" (Matt. 6:13). The common element in all these references is that the evil one is a power against which our faith does battle. The enemy cannot stand against the power of the Christian's faith.

Some cautions are needed in our understanding of Satan:

1. Satan, as an evil being, must not be understood as a creation of God. To do so would put a contradiction in God, and would make God the author of sin and evil. Such an idea cannot be squared with the biblical witness or tolerated by Christian faith. "God saw all that he had made, and it was very good" (Gen. 1:31).

2. But equally unacceptable is the dualistic idea that the devil

has always existed. God is not God if He has a polar opposite who is in any way on a comparable level. The Church has always rejected dualism, appealing to such scriptures as 2 Pet. 2:4 and Jude 6 and Jewish tradition reflected there, that Satan is a fallen angel. This, of course, raises other difficult questions, such as how sin could happen in a sinless heaven. But the "fallen angel" tradition has the value of making clear that Satan once was not. Furthermore, according to the Book of Revelation, he will finally be destroyed.

3. The idea of Satan as a fallen angel does not affect the understanding of sin that is revealed elsewhere throughout the Bible. If an angel sinned in heaven, he did so by misusing his freedom, just as any of us do when we sin. Thus, belief in Satan as a fallen angel may not tell us much about Satan himself, but it throws light on the meaning of sin. Sin originates in the misuse (or sometimes the disuse) of God-given freedom.

4. Taking the fallen angel idea a step further, if an angel—a purely spiritual being without a physical body and its accompanying desires that may become occasions of sin in human beings—could sin, then we see that sin is not basically rooted in the body. Instead, sin is a matter of spirit.

5. Satan is not the cause of our sinning. He tempts and entices us to sin. But no sinner can ever truthfully say, "The devil made me do it." To say that is to excuse oneself and avoid taking personal responsibility. If something or someone *made* me sin, then I am not the sinner, but rather that something or someone is. The Bible never lets us "off the hook" that easily. Satan's power may be great, but it's never irresistible. We're told to "resist the devil, and he will flee from you" (James 4:7). Martin Luther's time-honored hymn "A Mighty Fortress Is Our God" says it well:

> *The prince of darkness grim—*
> *We tremble not for him.*
> *His rage we can endure,*
> *For, lo, his doom is sure;*
> *One little word shall fell him.*

━━━

See also
   Angels
   Hell

ANGELS

During the television seasons of the past several years, viewers have been visited by a host of angels—although not necessarily a *heavenly* host! At least we can credit the television industry for being willing to gingerly treat some religious themes, even if their "orthodoxy" sometimes has left a bit to be desired.

Since I have never, as far as I know, been literally "touched by an angel," I am no authority on the subject. Therefore I cannot say if all angels sing and talk like Della Reese and are as sweet as Roma Downey, or if the "Angel of Death" is as gentle in real life (or real death) as he is on the screen. And I don't know if angels regularly appear in the real "Promised Land." Still, it's nice having something on television besides an overdose of sex and violence.

Unfortunately (or maybe fortunately), the Bible does not give us much concrete information about angels. Well, "concrete" may be the wrong word here—you can buy concrete angels at those roadside statuary shops that I often see in the Ozarks, where I sometimes go to get away from it all. Anyway, although the Bible says a lot about angels, what it says is not easily systematized.

Sometimes the Bible is unclear whether angels are ethereal beings or humans in a certain role. For example, Lot's two visitors are called "angels" in Gen. 19:1, but a few lines later (vv. 10 and 12) they're called "men." Which were they—men or angels? In some Christian art and hymnody, Jacob is portrayed as wrestling with an angel, but in Gen. 32:24 it is a "man." Then when the wrestling match is over, the "man" informs Jacob that he has been wrestling with God! Things get even more complicated when we read that the devil has angels too (Matt. 25:41). The Book of Revelation tells us that each of the seven churches of Asia had an "angel," which probably means the pastor of the church.

So what (or who) are angels? Both the Hebrew and Greek words for "angel" simply mean "messenger." In Heb. 1:14 angels are called "ministering spirits." Whatever (or whoever) they are, they are messengers who minister. Maybe sometimes human beings fill that role. And maybe there's an order of extra-human spiritual be-ings in God's vast creation whose service is to minister both to God and to His children.

Whoever (or whatever) they are, there are some cautions that should be observed in our understanding of angels:

1. Angels are not mediators of salvation. "There is one God and one mediator between God and men, the man Christ Jesus" (1 Tim. 2:5). An elaborate theory of angels, such as the Jews devel-oped during their exile in Babylon, runs the danger of putting an-gels in an intervening position between God and us. This danger prompted the author of Hebrews to proclaim that the Son was greater than the angels and that we have direct access to God through Jesus Christ.

2. Angels are not examples for us. We are not commanded to imitate the angels. (After all, according to one tradition, based loosely on a few scattered texts and augmented by poets like Milton and Dante, a third of the angels sinned and fell from heaven.) Jesus is our only example.

3. Belief in angels must not supplant belief in the work of the Holy Spirit. When conscious of being guided and guarded by a di-vine Presence, we must be careful lest we ascribe to the angels that which is really the Spririt's work, thus putting an extra layer of in-sulation between us and God.

On the positive side, belief in angels has value in teaching us that God's creation is vast and rich. If God has other orders of in-telligent beings, besides human creatures, it only exalts the wonder of God's creation and the power of the Creator. Related to that is the further consideration that belief in angels makes us aware that we're not alone in the universe. When we feel alone, there is com-fort in the Psalmist's assurance that "the angel of the LORD encamps around those who fear him, and he delivers them" (Ps. 34:7). In such times, perhaps we can experience what it really means to be "touched by an angel."

See also
    Creation

ADAM

To understand Adam is to understand ourselves.

In a famous line in the now-defunct comic strip *Pogo*, the little opossum says to the other animals in the swamp: "We have met the enemy, and it is us!"

That goes for Adam also. We have met him, and he is us. All of us! Adam's story could well be titled "Your Story and Mine."

In the Book of Genesis, Adam is the name of the first man created by God. But the Hebrew word *adham*, which is transliterated "Adam," occurs more than 550 times in the Old Testament, and in the majority of those cases it refers not to the first human being, but to humanity as a whole. And in the New Testament Adam is mentioned only three times in a purely "historical" way—as the first of all human creatures (see Luke 3:38; Jude 14; 1 Tim. 2:13-14). Elsewhere Adam is spoken of in a "representative" or "theological" way, specifically by Paul.

The word "Adam" is related to the Hebrew word *adamah*, which means "the ground" or "the earth." In Gen. 2:4-24, God forms man from the dust of the ground, breathes into his nostrils the breath of life, and he becomes a living being. Gen. 2:7 is the central affirmation of the biblical view of humanity: Human beings are animated bodies. They are body *and* spirit.

That we are made from the dust signifies the precariousness of our existence—we are just a heartbeat away from becoming dust once more! But there is another aspect to our creatureliness. Adam (humanity) was made in God's image (Gen. 1:27) and given dominion over all other creatures. There is thus something paradoxical about our existence, as the psalmist recognizes: On one hand, humanity was made "a little lower than God" and "crowned . . . with glory and honor" (Ps. 8:5, NRSV). On the other hand, we're made "like the animals that perish" (Ps. 49:12, 20, NRSV). In regard to human nature, biblical realism stands in sharp contrast both to a rosy optimism on the one hand and a cynical pessimism on the other.

A sad thing happened to Adam—and to us—on the way to the

fulfillment of a good Creator's bright promise of good creation. Sin entered the picture. Whence came sin? There is nothing to be gained by probing back behind the free will, the power of choice, with which humanity is endowed. Adam (humanity) simply chose, and chooses, to misuse this God-given freedom. Indeed, we have met the enemy—and it is us!

But there's another Adam who is not our enemy but our Friend! Paul speaks not only of "the first Adam" but also of "the last Adam" (1 Cor. 15:45). And that brings us to a brighter chapter in the Adam story—this story that is "your story and mine."

The Bible knows both the wretchedness of our sinful condition and the high destiny that is ours through the redemption made possible by Christ, who is "the last Adam." "For as in Adam all die, so in Christ all will be made alive" (1 Cor. 15:22). In Rom. 5:12-21 and 1 Cor. 15, Paul draws a sharp contrast between the two Adams. Adam yielded to temptation; Christ overcame it. Adam ushered in the old age; Christ inaugurated the new age. Through the disobedience of the first Adam, death entered the world; through the obedience of Christ, the last Adam, we may be made righteous. In the Garden of Eden, Adam and Eve said in essence, "Not your will but mine be done." In another garden called Gethsemane, the last Adam prayed, "Not my will, but yours be done" (Luke 22:42). In Eden the first Adam, influenced by Eve, grasped for equality with God (Gen. 3:5); in Gethsemane the Last Adam, who already had equality with God, "did not consider equality with God a thing to be grasped, but made himself nothing, taking the very nature of a servant" (Phil. 2:6-7).

Yes, we have met the first Adam—and he is us. His story is our story. We have also met Christ, the last Adam. He is our Friend, and by His grace His story can become our story too. To understand the first Adam is to understand ourselves as we existed in sin. To understand Christ, the last Adam, is to understand ourselves as we will be, for "we know that when he appears, we shall be like him" (1 John 3:2).

See also
   Sin
   Woman

WOMAN

As the women's liberation movement began to pick up steam a few decades ago, some people quipped, "Women have come a long way—all the way from Adam's rib to women's lib!"

And so they have. Now, I'm not a disciple of the women's liberation movement in its more radical expressions. But neither am I an advocate of male superiority (and female submission) on the basis of some biblical interpretations that are highly suspect. It is the latter point of view that I wish to address here. Advocates of male superiority have advanced the following myths, supposedly based on the Genesis creation accounts:

Myth 1. *Woman is subordinate to man because man was created first.* If this is valid, then man must be subordinate to the animals, for they were created before man! Sometimes men sink to the level of animals, but they weren't created that way.

Myth 2. *Woman is subordinate to man because she was made from man.* True, the creation account in Gen. 2 says God took a rib from Adam's side with which to make Eve. But if this proves women's subordination, then men must be subordinate to dust, for "the LORD God formed the man from the dust of the ground" (v. 7). Not many men would like to think of themselves as subordinate to dirt, although some of us may act like clods!

Myth 3. *Woman is subordinate to man because God created her to be man's helper* (Gen. 2:18). This reflects a cultural bias that considers a helper as someone lower on the scale than the one who is being helped, as some kind of "assistant" to the big boss. If this were valid, then one could argue that the triune God is subordinate to human beings. In the Old Testament particularly in the Psalms, God is referred to as "our Helper." The Hebrew word *ezer* used in the creation account of Gen. 2 is the same word used elsewhere in the Old Testament to describe God as Israel's "helper." In 1 John 2:1, Jesus Christ is called the *Paraclete*, which may be translated "Helper." And in John's Gospel, chapters 14—16, Jesus refers several times to the promised Holy Spirit as our *Paraclete*, which is translated "Helper" in the *New American Standard Bible*. In each of these cases, it is the greater who helps the lesser. Thus, for God to create the woman to be man's helper does not mean she is subordinate to the man. In the creation account in Gen. 1:26-30, both man and woman are created in the image of God at the same time. Both are given dominion over the rest of creation, and both are blessed. There is no hierarchy or subordination.

Myth 4. *Woman is subordinate to man because God said to her, "He will rule over you" (Gen. 3:16).* But God said this because of the sin of the first pair. Men ruling over women is the result of the Fall. It is part of the curse, one very striking manifestation of sin. If it were God's will in Creation for woman to be ruled by man, what point would there be to the curse?

The final answer to these and other myths is in Christ's attitude toward women and in Paul's words in Eph. 5:22-33, in which the apostle admonishes wives to submit to their husbands. But he places an even greater responsibility on the husbands. They are to "love their wives" (v. 25). And they are to love them "just as Christ loved the church and gave himself up for her" (v. 25). That's a big order! It gets even bigger: "Husbands ought to love their wives as their own bodies. He who loves his wife loves himself" (v. 28).

How can that be? When a man and a woman marry, they become "one flesh" (Gen. 2:24). Paul does insist on submission. But it's a *mutual* submission. Husband and wife are to be submissive to each other, for they're one.

Paul affirms that it's God's intention for human beings to live as equal partners: "There is neither . . . male nor female, for you are all one in Christ Jesus" (Gal. 3:28). Women were the first witnesses of Christ's resurrection. Jesus commanded them to go and proclaim the good news to the men (Mark 16:7). Who are we to forbid them?

Let us all—men and women alike—be done with the myths!

See also
   Feminism

FEMINISM

T he 20th century was characterized in advanced societies by a growing feminism. It might be said that this trend was a reaction to the lack of respect accorded women in the past. Thus, contemporary feminism finds its roots in the absence of true respect for womanhood, which has characterized much of human history—even much of Christian history.

Revealed truth as found in Scripture and in the life and ministry of Christ teaches us something different. Respect for woman, amazement at the mystery of womanhood, and finally the love of God himself and of Christ as expressed in the scheme of redemption are all elements that have never been completely absent in the faith and life of the Church. This can be seen in a rich tradition of customs and practices that, regrettably, is nowadays being eroded. In our civilization, woman has become largely an object of pleasure.

It is very significant, on the other hand, that in the midst of this very situation an authentic theology of woman is being reborn. The spiritual beauty, the particular genius of women is being rediscovered. The basis for the consolidation of the position of women in life, not only family life but also social and cultural life, are being redefined. The proper significance of womanhood in the Christian religion is shown in the respect Jesus had for women, the apostle Paul's admonitions about mutual submission of husband and wife to each other, and his words that husbands are to love their wives "just as Christ loved the church and gave himself up for her" (Eph. 5:25).

A new look at Mary, the mother of Jesus, might help Protestants recover a healthy respect for women.

In the early centuries a great debate took place between the church at Alexandria and the church at Constantinople, two centers of power in the Church that were rivals to each other. Cyril of Alexandria and other Alexandrians affirmed Mary as *theotokos*, which came to be translated (somewhat incorrectly) as "mother of God." At Constantinople, the patriarch Nestorius disagreed, taking the position that Mary could not be called "mother of God" but was simply the mother of the human Jesus.

At first glance, most Protestants would perhaps tend to side with Nestorius and be horrified to think that Mary could be referred to as the mother of God. And yet it should be asked of all who deny the *theotokos* doctrine, "Do you mean to claim that the child who came forth from Mary's womb was *not* in any way God?" That puts a different face on the issue! Besides, *theotokos* is best translated not as "mother of God" but as "bearer of God." Mary is the one who gave birth to the one who is God.

At the Council of Calcedon in A.D. 451, the Church mediated the issue by affirming that Mary was "mother of God" but immediately added the words "as regards his manhood." It was an ingenious compromise. It was also a necessary one if we're to accord proper respect to Mary and at the same time avoid deifying her. After all, what Mary bore was God in human flesh. But at the same time, she was herself in need of redemption, as shown by her presence in the Upper Room on the Day of Pentecost, waiting for the promised outpouring of the Holy Spirit (Acts 1:14).

But back to the present day. Mary cannot be a model for women if she is deified and seen as a co-redeemer along with Christ. Certainly the papal claims of her immaculate conception, perpetual virginity, and bodily assumption have no basis in biblical revelation. No other woman could in any way follow such a pattern. By exalting Mary too highly, we place her out of reach for other women. No woman could emulate such a pattern.

But she can provide a beautiful model for women if seen in her utter humanness—one that's completely open to God. Mary's is a humanness that, in spite of the seeming impossibility of what has been told her by the angel, can say in complete obedience, "I am the Lord's servant. . . . May it be to me as you have said" (Luke 1:38).

Believing that veneration of Mary detracts from the centrality of Christ, Protestants have often neglected her unduly. But the increasing importance of women's issues has spurred new interest in Mary among Catholics and Protestants alike. Only good can come from that.

See also
Woman

SIN

T he third chapter of Genesis (the story of the Fall) gives us a graphic picture of sin. We would err if we thought it to be merely the story of Adam and Eve. It is "your story and mine"—the story of us all. To see what sin was in the lives of the first pair is to see what it is in *every* human being. In fact, the Hebrew word translated "Adam" in this chapter is also translated "man" in some of the verses. It can simply mean "human being." To read the story as if it applied only to Adam and Eve is to ignore our responsibility and to fail to understand what sin does in our own lives.

In the story of the Fall, *sin begins in a questioning of divine authority.* The serpent asked, "Did God really say . . . ?" Eve's mistake was to take her cues from a creature (one "more crafty than any of the wild animals that the LORD God had made" [Gen. 3:1]) instead of from the Creator. Later the apostle Paul would write of all the sons of Adam and daughters of Eve: "They . . . worshipped and served created things rather than the Creator" (Rom. 1:25).

The book of Genesis presents *sin as essentially the attempt to become like God.* That was the serpent's promise: "When you eat . . . you will be like God, knowing good and evil" (Gen. 3:5). Here the serpent told the truth, for later (in v. 22), God confirms it, saying, "The man has now become like one of us, knowing good and evil."

How does one become like God by sinning? The one who really knows good and evil is the one who determines what they are. God is the one who makes the definitions, who says what is good and what is evil. But Eve seized for herself the right to do the defining. "She saw that the fruit . . . was good" (v. 6). *That* is how one becomes like God by sinning—by making a grab for final authority. By seeking to be the sovereign instead of the steward of God's creation, as each person is meant to be (1:28-30).

But *sin also has a social dimension.* The woman gave fruit to her husband and he ate it. If "misery loves company," as the saying goes, so does sin! In Eve's offer, and Adam's acceptance, sin was "transmitted" from person to person, before there was any conception or birth of children. Sin is not something written into the genetic code, found in DNA molecules. If it were, our genetic scientists might eventually rid the human race of it. That would be nice, but let's not count on it!

Sin involves the breaking of fellowship. When the man and woman saw their nakedness, they were ashamed as they had not been before they sinned (Gen. 2:25). They attempted to hide from one another by making coverings for themselves (Gen. 3:7). They also tried to hide from God among the trees of the garden (v. 8).

Sin includes the denial of responsibility. When confronted with his deed, Adam blamed Eve. In so doing, he blamed God, saying, "The woman you put here with me" is responsible (Gen. 3:12). Then when God confronted Eve, she said, "The serpent deceived me" (v. 13). Neither the man nor the woman would accept responsibility for their deeds. Still today, sin is the deluding notion that something else (society, parents, heredity, environment) besides our own choice caused us to sin.

Sin robs life of meaning and purpose. The woman is told her pains in childbearing will increase. Because sin is in the world, parenting still has its pains and agonies, which dilute the joys of rearing children. The man is told that painful toil will be his lot as he makes his living by the sweat of his brow. As a rule (though not a universal one), men can express their creativity in their work, and women can express theirs in motherhood. Both realms of creativity are impaired because of sin.

Finally, *the end result of sin is alienation from God.* Adam and Eve are banished from the Garden, and cheribim are placed at the gate with a flaming sword to prevent their return. To live in sin is to live outside of God. To be bound to self is to be free from God, but freedom from God is death.

No wonder the apostle Paul could say that "in Adam all die" (1 Cor. 15:22).

See also
  Adam
  Temptation

INCARNATION

T he word *incarnation* is derived from the Latin *carnis* ("flesh") and means "becoming flesh," as in John 1:14, referring to the act whereby God became man in Jesus of Nazareth. God's visit to His own creation is the supreme example of a divine intervention in the affairs of humanity.

The theological development of this doctrine reached its apex at the Council of Chalcedon, in A.D. 451. Here the Church declared that Jesus Christ is "truly God and truly man.' How can that be?

In a theology class one day, discussing the Incarnation, I drew two figures on the chalkboard, leaving some space between them. On the left I drew an outline of a man, and on the right I drew a circle to represent God. Of course, no one can draw God, but the circle was a weak attempt to represent the ultimate reality. I then said that any students who wished could come to the board and draw their conception of Christ between the two drawings on the board. Several students made the attempt. Interestingly, each drawing portrayed one of the heresies taught in the early centuries!

In the center one student drew a duplicate of the figure on the left and said, "Jesus was just like us.' I pointed out that the ancient heretics known as Ebionites agreed. Someone else used dotted lines to draw a man and then, with solid lines, drew a circle at his heart, saying, "Jesus only looked like a man, but He was really God." This sounded like the ancient Docetists, who held that Jesus only appeared human but actually was not. Another drew a circle, placing beneath it a man's torso and legs, saying, "He was part man, but God was the 'head,' so to speak." This was what the Apollinarian heretics taught, as well as the Monophysites and Monothelites. A young woman drew a man superimposed over the circle and split the whole drawing down the middle, making Jesus half man and half God. I compared this to the Arians. Someone else drew a man with a circle stuck to his side, like two beings glued together. This was Nestorianism.

The class thus became a microcosm of the Early Church as it

tried to explain the Incarnation. Each view that was proposed back then had some strength but also a fatal flaw, and the Church would get together and say, "No, that's not it."

As the class continued to discuss the issue, they came to see that if Jesus were *only* human, we would have to say that humanity saved itself by producing a perfect man. But if Jesus were *only* God who looked like a man, He would not have experienced what being human was all about, and there would have been no real Incarnation.

So the only adequate conclusion the class, as well as the Early Church, could reach was this: "Jesus Christ is truly God, and He is truly man." And that does not add up to *two* different people, one divine and one human. Nor is it adequate to say that Jesus was one composite person made up of something divine and something human, sort of a half-and-half being.

What the Incarnation means is simply this: We can point to the historical Jesus and say, "He is God." At the same time, we can point to the very same person and say, "He is a man"—not merely "man" in some general way, but *a* particular man, a first-century Jew subject to all the conditions of living in this world. Everything we mean when we say "human" applies to Jesus. (Here we must remember that true humanity is sinless humanity; that sin is not an essential ingredient of human nature, but always a distortion of it.) Jesus was the perfect example of humanness. And everything that God is, Jesus is. In answer to the question "What does it mean to be human?" Christian faith answers, "Jesus." And in answer to the question "What is God like?" Christian faith answers, "Jesus."

An adequate doctrine of salvation requires both affirmations. He must be divine, or His life, death, and resurrection are not God's saving action in the world. And He must be a human being, or His saving action is not within the world of our human affairs, and has nothing to do with us.

There is mystery here. It is an affirmation of faith. It takes our minds as far as they can go to say it, but we have to say, "Jesus is truly God and truly man."

See also
  Atonement

ATONEMENT

We may gain insight into the meaning of "atonement" by breaking the English word down as *at-one-ment*. Thus, it has to do with "being in accord," or bringing together, two estranged parties. Sin breaks relationship with God, but God's gracious love restores the possibility of having the relationship restored.

The Atonement is a supreme mystery. Why was it necessary for the sinless Son of God to die such an ignoble death in order for our sins to be forgiven? Why couldn't God merely inspire the prophets and apostles to tell us we were forgiven?

It is significant that there has never been an "official" theory or explanation of the Atonement adopted by any church council or inscribed in any of the historic creeds. What we have are attempts, both in the New Testament and in the history of doctrine, to view the Cross from different angles and describe it in various images or models that are more like illustrations than explanations.

In his book *The Story of God*, Michael Lodahl discusses four major atonement models he finds in the New Testament, namely, Jesus as prince, priest, prophet, and presence. The first three were delineated by Swedish theologian Gustaf Aulén early in the 20th century, although he used different terms and discussed them in the order of their appearance in history.

The first model is Jesus as *Prince*, who *liberates* us from the bondage of sin. Because of sin, humanity is captive of Satan. Humanity is unable to free itself from the prison of sin. On the Cross, Jesus, whom Aulén calls *Christus Victor*, won a decisive victory over Satan, sin, oppression, rebellion, and apathy. Jesus the Prince, the Son of the King, is the royal Fighter who comes to our rescue, breaks down the prison walls, and frees us from all that oppresses us. This model was appropriate for the first few Christian centuries in which oppression by Roman armies, as well as by inner demonic forces, was widespread. It has been equally appropriate in the 20th century, when sin's effects have been seen as oppression, addiction, and violence. Jesus the victorious Prince is the only deliverer.

Jesus as *Priest* is the *propitiation* for our sin. To propitiate a person is to appease, to win over, or to avert that person's anger. This model suggests that human beings owe complete obedience to God, but because of their sin against an infinite God, they are incapable of giving such obedience and thus have incurred an infinite moral debt. God could not lightly cancel the debt. The debt must be paid by human beings, since they incurred it, but only God was capable of paying it. So God became human in Christ so that as a human He could pay the debt that humanity owed. As the sinless God-Man, He was able to do so. This model became appropriate during the Middle Ages and the age of feudalism, in which everyone must "satisfy" the demands of those in authority, whether he or she be emperor, pope, bishop, knight, or landlord. Calvinists modify this model to suggest that Christ's death was not the payment of our debt to God, but the punishment for our sins that Christ takes upon himself. But the idea of punishment is not the best category under which to understand the Cross.

Jesus as *Prophet* is the *Reconciler*, who both speaks and lives God's reconciling word to humanity. This model declares that Jesus' death on the Cross was a demonstration of God's love, which is able to dispel our fear of God and inspire our hearts to love both God and neighbor.

Lodahl finds a fourth model, namely Jesus as the *Presence*, which focuses on the New Testament concept of *participation*. This emphasis has been especially prominent in Eastern Christianity. In this model, atonement is brought about not by Christ's death alone, but by the Incarnation as a whole. The Incarnation is the "enfleshment" of God, of God's descent into human finitude and suffering, even to the point of death. By taking human nature upon himself, God in Christ redeems it.

These four models do not exhaust the meaning of Calvary. It is fortunate that the Church never adopted any one of them as "official." The wonder of the Cross is such that in any age, as the historical and social conditions change, the theology of Atonement may be described by the use of images and models that are meaningful within the context of those conditions.

See also
  Incarnation

RESURRECTION

Easter is a time when the theme "resurrection" is central in the Church's worship. But in reality, our worship on every Lord's Day is a celebration of the truth that Christ was raised from the dead on "the first day of the week."

Christian faith confesses, in the words of the Apostles' Creed, "I believe in . . . the resurrection of the body." Resurrection is a trustworthy description of our future, because it has already happened in history. Christ's resurrection is the central event of the New Testament, which gave birth to the Christian faith.

For Paul, Christ's resurrection presupposes a general resurrection at the end of history (1 Cor. 15:16) of which Christ's resurrection is the "firstfruits" (vv. 20-23). In raising Jesus from the dead, God demonstrated His purpose to raise others who have been united with Christ through faith. The link between His resurrection and ours is indicated in passages such as John 5:25-26; Rom. 6:4-5; and 1 Pet. 1:3-4. Jesus was the *first* one to be raised, but He will not be the *only* one!

What can we learn about the nature of *our* resurrection from the fact of *His*? Christian faith has steadfastly proclaimed that the *body* will be raised. The Apostles' Creed does not tie belief in "the life everlasting" to the idea of the immortality of the soul, but rather to faith in "the resurrection of the body." Pagan Greek philosophy was dualistic, teaching that the real essence of the person was the soul. All matter was considered to be evil, the physical body being a prison in which the soul was trapped during its sojourn in this earthly life. The soul alone was immortal and untouchable by death.

In contrast to this dualism, biblical thought sees the person as a unity. It has been said that a body without a soul is a corpse, but a soul without a body is a ghost. Life after death means the resurrection of the whole person. In the New Testament, only God is essentially immortal (1 Tim. 6:15). When we human beings are spoken of as having immortality, it is derivative, something that we "put on" (1 Cor. 15:53-54, NRSV) or with which we must be "clothed"

(NIV). It is not something we already possess by nature but is a gift of grace made possible by Christ's own resurrection from the dead. (John 5:28-29 and Acts 24:15 seem to teach that even the wicked will be raised from the dead in order to be judged.)

The resurrected life is continuous with the life we have here and now as believers who have been buried with Christ in baptism and raised to new life (Rom. 6:4). Paul tells us that God "made us alive with Christ" and "raised us up" with Him (Eph. 2:5-6). Our resurrection is both realized and future, both "already" and "not yet."

As for the future aspect, Paul speaks of the resurrected body as a "spiritual body" (1 Cor. 15:44). In this earthly existence, since our bodies are physical, we cannot fully know what a spiritual body is. Whatever it is, it will enable us to know and communicate with one another in the future state, just as this physical body enables us to do so in the physical world. Certainly the body of the risen Jesus, whatever it is like, enabled Him to communicate with and be recognized by the disciples in the Upper Room. His risen body is different from His pre-Easter body; sometimes He was not even recognized by those who had known Him in the flesh. Thus, there was discontinuity. But there was also continuity; they could see His nail scars.

Do we come forth as spiritual bodies immediately after death, or must we await the Last Day and Christ's Second Coming? One can find biblical proof-texts that seem to validate either position. But we know this: If we live and die *in Christ*, we go to be *with Christ*. It is also our destiny to be *like Christ*, with a resurrection body like His. Whether or not our Christian loved ones who have died are already *like Christ* in that sense, we can rest assured that they are now *with Christ*. The chronological details are not the main point of our Christian hope. In any case, it is Christ who awaits us in death, and it is Christ who awaits us at the end of the age.

His resurrection is the best clue to our own. "Now we are children of God, and what we will be has not yet been made known"— except for this: "we shall be like him" (1 John 3:2).

See also
Death
Glorification
Time

GRACE

The word "grace" represents the foundation of our relationship to God. What is grace? One of the oldest definitions (so old that no one knows where it came from or who first proposed it) is "God's unmerited favor." The key word is "unmerited," that is, undeserved. Because of sin and its effects, grace is undeserved but drastically needed by all human beings.

I once heard a well-known theologian lecture on grace. He told of a friend of his from Michigan who was motoring to Florida and stopped at a restaurant in Georgia to eat breakfast. He ordered a typical American breakfast—eggs, bacon, toast, and coffee. When the waitress set the plate before him, he asked her, "What's this glob of white stuff on my plate?" "Grits," the waitress replied. He protested: "I didn't order grits." And she replied, "That's correct, Sir. Down here you don't order them, and you don't pay for them—they just come."

After telling that story, the lecturer remarked, "That's what grace is—we didn't order it, and we don't pay for it, but we get it anyway. It just comes. Grace is grits, and grits is grace!" An amusing analogy, but not bad. Not bad at all.

The Bible from beginning to end is a book about grace. It's a mistake to think the Old Testament is only a book of Law and the New Testament a book of grace. Creation itself is an act of divine grace. The giving of the Law and the institution of sacrifices were all for the purpose of pointing people toward a salvation they needed but did not deserve. In short, they were acts of grace.

But for the Christian, grace is centered in Jesus Christ. Jesus is "the face of grace." Divine grace is not confined to the life and work of Jesus, but it is defined by that life and work. "The law was given through Moses; grace . . . came by Jesus Christ" (John 1:17).

We gain insight into the meaning of grace when we note that in New Testament Greek the word charis (grace) is related to the word charisma (gift). Thus, grace has a gift-like character. It always comes as something we did not deserve, did not purchase, did not earn. The benefits of grace come to us as a divine gift. "For by grace you have been saved through faith, and this is not your own doing; it is the gift of God" (Eph. 2:8, NRSV).

Since grace is the gift of God, and since God is sovereign, we cannot control grace. We cannot program it, predict it, or corral it. We cannot say, "Lo, here" or "Lo, there." When we think it will come from the east, it comes from the west. When we think it will come from the north, it comes from the south. Grace is full of surprises. It ceases to be grace when it ceases to be "amazing" grace!

Grace is free. It transcends every legalistic way of thinking, every system of moral bookkeeping, every calculation of rewards and penalties; no tariff can be imposed on it. It is God's doing, and it is marvelous to behold.

Wesleyans often speak of "prevenient grace." The word "prevenient" means literally "to come before" (from the Latin *prae*, before, and *venire*, to come), hence "preceding." In theology, the term refers to the grace of God that comes before salvation, or the grace that we are given even before we respond to God in faith.

This does not mean, however, that there are different kinds of grace, as if the grace before we're saved is a different kind of grace from the grace by which, and after which, we're saved. There's a continuity of grace; it's all of one piece. In one sense, all grace is prevenient. All of God's saving action precedes our own response. Long before we ever believed, even before we were born or conceived, God did what He needed to do to bring about our salvation. That's what grace means. Every Christian, then, can gratefully sing with Charles Wesley,

> *Plenteous grace with Thee is found,*
> *Grace to cover all my sin.*
> *Let the healing streams abound;*
> *Make and keep me pure within.*
> *Thou of life the Fountain art;*
> *Freely let me take of Thee.*
> *Spring Thou up within my heart;*
> *Rise to all eternity.*

See also
Faith
Works

FAITH

Salvation is "by grace," but it comes to us "through faith" (Eph. 2:8). Faith is the human response that allows grace to do its full work in us.

What *is* faith? When asked by his Sunday School teacher to define faith, a boy replied, "It's believing something's true when you know it isn't so."

He was completely wrong, but skeptics sometimes seem to think that's what we Christians are doing. In this modern age, they say, Christians surely know better than to believe in God and the Bible, but they go to church on Sundays pretending that it's all true. If that's what faith is, surely the believer is in trouble!

Sometimes faith is contrasted with knowledge. Some things we know to be true, and some things we just believe to be true. For example, we know that in outer space are many other planets besides our own. Some people believe there's life on some of those planets. Now suppose we finally learn that there really is life on some far-off planet, then that which was only *believed* will have become *known*. Faith will have given way to knowledge. This implies that the more knowledge we attain, the less faith we need and that faith is inferior to knowledge. If that's what faith is, once again the believer is in trouble! But this is not the concept of faith expressed by Paul when he says that knowledge will pass away, but faith remains (1 Cor. 13:8, 13). Faith, then, in its biblical meaning is not something inferior to knowledge.

Sometimes the word faith is understood in the sense of *"the* faith," that is, the whole body of truth that has come down to us through the historic Christian tradition, "the faith that was once for all entrusted to the saints" (Jude 3). This understanding is certainly valid; there *is* an objective deposit of truth that constitutes the intellectual content of the Christian religion. But it's a subtle step from this valid understanding to the invalid idea that saving faith is merely an intellectual assent to this body of truth. James tells us that even the demons have this kind of faith (James 2:19).

Although there is an intellectual content to faith, the faith through which one is saved is more than that. It is personal trust in God. As such, it is a way of knowing. To have faith in God is to know Him—not merely to know *about* Him. It is a knowledge that is more than intellectual; it is an intimate personal knowledge by which a person is willing to put his or her trust in God.

The Hebrews, more than the Greeks, understood knowledge this way. For them, knowledge was not a mere collection of facts in the head nor a grasp of abstract principles. Knowledge was personal, or better, *inter*personal. Interestingly, the Hebrews described the sexual union of man and wife as a "knowing" ("Adam knew Eve his wife; and she conceived, and bare Cain," Gen. 4:1, KJV). So to have faith in God is to *know* Him, personally and intimately, after the analogy of two people knowing each other in the marriage bond.

The faith through which we're saved is not merely "believing *that*," but "believing *in*." I may believe *that* there is life on other planets, and I may believe *that* God exists. Of course, one who comes to God must, as a minimum, "believe that he exists" (Heb. 11:6). But salvation comes when we believe *in* God, putting our complete trust *in* Him. When we confess our faith in the words of the Apostles' Creed, we do *not* say, "I believe *that* God exists," but rather we affirm our trust in Him by saying, "I believe *in* God the Father Almighty."

That's the kind of faith described by the writer of the Epistle to the Hebrews at the beginning of his "roll call" of the heroes of faith: "Now faith is being sure of what we hope for and certain of what we do not see" (Heb. 11:1).

> *Lord give us such a faith as this;*
> *And then, whate'er may come,*
> *We'll taste, e'en here, the hallowed bliss*
> *Of an eternal home.*
> —William H. Bathurst

See also
Grace
Works

WORKS

S ince Paul says we are saved "not by works" (Eph. 2:9), we must not misunderstand the place of good works in the Christian life. Three wrong conclusions could be drawn from the truth that salvation is "by grace through faith.'

First, a person could incorrectly say, "Since we're saved by grace and not by anything we do, then *I can do nothing about it*. God grants salvation or He doesn't. Either way, it's His decision, not mine. Nothing I do will make any difference." This conclusion could logically be drawn from the doctrine of absolute predestination or unconditional election. Of course, believers know that our good works are not something for which we can take credit. We know we're unworthy of the gift of salvation. But the gift of salvation by grace does not eliminate our own responsibility. Paul admonished, "Work out your salvation with fear and trembling," emphasizing human responsibility, and then he immediately added, "for it is God who works in you to will and to act according to his good purpose" (Phil. 2:12-13).

A second erroneous conclusion could be "Since I'm saved by grace, and not by anything I do, then *I don't need to do anything at all*." This is a form of what is known as "quietism," which teaches that the believer is relieved of the necessity of doing good works. Certainly good works are not a means of earning salvation, but this does not mean they have no value. Good works are the *fruit* of salvation, not its *root*. As Martin Luther said in his *Treatise on Christian Liberty*, "Good works do not make a good man, but a good man does good works."

A third wrong conclusion could be "Since I'm saved by grace and not by works, then *I can do anything I please*." This is the error known as antinomianism (Gr. *anti* = against; *nomos* = law), which holds that grace has freed us from the necessity of keeping the law of God. This conclusion could logically be drawn from the doctrine of "eternal security" or "once saved, always saved." Since we're saved by grace as a gift, our salvation has no relation to anything we do. But the true Christian never says, "Anything goes." To do so would be what Dietrich Bonhoeffer called "cheap grace." Paul was combating cheap grace when he said, "Shall we go on sinning so that grace may increase? By no means!" (Rom. 6:1-2). Grace is free, but it is not cheap.

Works are never meritorious. That is, they do not earn us anything before God. God does not consider them as "brownie points" or "merit badges." John Wesley insisted that for salvation, faith was necessary immediately and directly but that good works (he called them "fruits meet for repentance," in the words of John the Baptist [Matt. 3:8, KJV]) are necessary only conditionally, if there be time and opportunity for them. "Otherwise," he said, "a man may be justified without them, as was the thief upon the cross" (*Works*, 6:48).

Some have thought there was a contradiction between Paul, who says we're "saved by grace . . . not by works" (Eph. 2:8-9) and James, who says "faith, if it has no works, is dead" (James 2:17, NASB). But clearly they are not speaking of faith in the same sense. James speaks of faith as intellectual assent and says even the demons have such faith (2:19). But Paul speaks of a faith that is fully persuaded that God has power to do what He has promised. Such faith God credits to us as righteousness (Rom. 4:1-6). What James means by "faith plus works" is not different from what Paul means by "faith alone."

One might wonder how the parable of the prodigal son would have ended if Jesus had carried it a little further. Would the prodigal, when he went to bed that night after feasting on stall-fed barbecued veal, have said to himself, "This is great! A full stomach and now clean sheets! Father didn't even say I had to work to pay off what I squandered. I think I'll just sleep in tomorrow morning"? No! He surely would have been up early and working in the fields, perhaps even before the elder brother got there. Not because he had to, but because the father's forgiveness had been so overwhelming he wanted to work for him out of sheer gratitude for the acceptance freely bestowed on him.

See also
   Faith
   Grace

CONVERSION

C onversion" is a rather slippery term. One can be "converted" *from* almost anything *to* almost anything else. But here we're interested in Christian conversion—what takes place when one becomes a Christian, when he or she converted from sin to salvation.

Three major terms depict the New Testament meaning of conversion: justification, regeneration, and adoption. They will be treated together here, because they cannot be distinguished chronologically or experientially. We are justified, regenerated, and adopted all at once. All are parts of Christian conversion, and we cannot distinguish them by looking into our hearts and analyzing our experience.

But we *can* distinguish them *theologically*, in terms of what God does for us when He saves us. In the one religious experience, He justifies, regenerates, and adopts us, and the three are distinctly different aspects of God's saving action.

Another reason the terms are treated together here is because they can best be understood by comparing and contrasting them with each other. We will begin with the first two.

"Justification" is a legal or judicial term from the language of the law court. In justification, we're acquitted of our guilt and treated as if we had never sinned. In justification, considered by itself, we're *declared* to be righteous, *not* actually *made* righteous.

But God justifies no one whom He does not also regenerate. If "justification" is a term derived from the courtroom, "regeneration" comes from the delivery room. It is a "family" term. It bespeaks the idea of birth, of a new life coming into existence. Regeneration and new birth are synonymous terms; to be regenerated means to be "born again." In regeneration we're not merely *declared* righteous— we're *made* righteous.

As noted, the terms can best be understood by contrasting them. Justification is what God does *for us* by His Son; regeneration is what God works *in us* by His Spirit. In justification we're saved from the *guilt* of sin; in regeneration we're saved from the *bondage* of sin, and the *power* of sin is broken.

The terms "justification," "regeneration," and "adoption" are metaphors, or illustrations. It's as if the New Testament writers, trying to describe what it means to be a Christian, cast about for suitable metaphors. In one sense, they would think, being a Christian is something like being acquitted in a courtroom trial. God the righteous Judge, who knows we're sinners, has pronounced the "not guilty" verdict and set us free. It's the father of the prodigal treating the son as if he had never left home. That's justification.

But that one metaphor does not say it all. In another sense, being a Christian is something like being born, or even (and here the metaphors get a bit mixed) like being raised from the dead. We who had no life or were dead in trespasses and sins have been brought to life by the life-giving Holy Spirit. Regeneration, or new birth, is a fitting metaphor. Interestingly, it is the most *feminine* of the biblical terms for salvation. In the human realm, giving birth is the act of a woman. This shows a "feminine" side of God. In regeneration, divine life is given to us by grace. Birth is always a gift; we never give birth to ourselves. We cannot enter into new life by our own effort but are totally dependent on God's "motherly" deliverance and nourishment. This is the new birth, or regeneration.

One metaphor alone would not carry all the meaning. Nor can the above two say it all. A third New Testament metaphor for conversion is *adoption*. This figure of speech is like justification in that it is a legal term. But adoption is, in another sense, like regeneration in that it is a "family" term. It says that we, who were once the children of the devil, have been adopted into God's family, where Christ is our elder brother and we are joint-heirs with Christ (Rom. 8:15-17; Gal. 4:4-7).

These three metaphors, then—justification, regeneration, and adoption—are the chief ones by which the New Testament writers attempt to tell us what it means to be a Christian.

See also
   Justification
   Regeneration
   Adoption

JUSTIFICATION

In Alice Walker's novel *The Color Purple*, Celia is shocked upon learning that her friend Shug thinks God loves her even if she does nothing for Him, like go to church, sing in the choir, or feed the preacher. Shug replies, "But if God love me, Celia, I don't have to do all that. Unless I want to" (176).

That's what the New Testament doctrine of justification is all about: We don't "have to" do anything to make God love us. But having accepted the fact that He loves us unconditionally, we will doubtless "want to" do what we can for Him, not to earn our acceptance but in gratitude for His mercy and grace.

The Christian life is grounded in the grace of God and is based in our union with Christ. Justification is the objective side of this relationship. Although the idea is expressed in a limited way in the Old Testament and also in the non-Pauline writings of the New Testament, it's the apostle Paul who develops the concept most thoroughly.

According to Paul, justification is received by faith and not by works (Rom. 3:23-24; 5:1). Accomplished by the sacrifice of Christ, it is our free, unconditional, and unmerited acceptance by God "who justifies the wicked" (Rom. 4:5). "Justification," a term from the judicial sphere, means "acquittal." That we are justified means that our guilt has been removed and our broken relationship with God has been restored by God's act of free grace and forgiveness.

Sometimes this doctrine is expressed in the abbreviated form "justification by faith." This would be a distortion if it were taken to mean that faith is a human act by which we earn our justification. A fuller and more accurate expression is Paul's statement in Eph. 2:8-9: "It is by grace you have been saved, through faith." To nail down the point even further, the apostle then adds, "This is not from yourselves, it is the gift of God—not by works, so that no one can boast." God's gift of justification is in no way dependent upon our works or our worthiness. Our reception of this gift depends only on our faith. But we cannot merit justification, even by

our faith. Faith is simply the proper response of trust and acceptance of God's unconditional acceptance of us. Justification is "the
acceptance of acceptance." We are justified when, in simple faith,
we accept the fact that we are accepted by God on the basis of the
atonement made by His only Son.

> In my hand no price I bring;
> Simply to Thy cross I cling.

Although Martin Luther called justification the doctrine by
which the Church stands or falls, the entire Christian understanding of salvation cannot be reduced to this single truth. Nevertheless, this doctrine has enormous relevance for our day. Consider the
many ways in which we try to justify ourselves, to make our lives
meaningful and acceptable, if not by "good works," at least by hard
work or by acts that we think will win the approval of others. The
desire for success and the quest for acceptance in our competitive
society often borders on idolatry. We become terrified by the
prospect of failing to win the love and recognition that we crave.
This attempt to gain the acceptance of others can easily transfer into our religious lives so that we try to become pleasing to God by
our own efforts.

Justification is the word the New Testament uses to assure us
that, with God, we are not "nobodies," but "somebodies." We are
somebodies because the God who is our Creator and Redeemer says
we are, because we are made in God's image and Jesus died for us.

In Rom. 4 Paul uses Abraham as the classic example of one who
was justified by grace through faith. "Abraham believed God, and it
was credited to him as righteousness" (v. 3). He was "fully persuaded that God had power to do what he had promised" (v. 21). Because of such faith, Abraham became the father of all of us "to
whom God will credit righteousness—for us who believe in him
who raised Jesus our Lord from the dead" (v. 24).

Shug was correct. If God loves us, we don't have to do anything—unless we want to. But we want to. Don't we?

See also
   Conversion
   Regeneration
   Adoption

REGENERATION

Whereas justification is the "objective" aspect of Christian conversion, regeneration may be called the "subjective" aspect. It refers to what God does *within* us, bestowing spiritual life to the repentant and believing sinner. "Regeneration" is a metaphor taken not from the field of law (as is the case with justification), but from the field of human biology and of family life.

Accordingly, "regeneration" is a synonym for the "new birth." The conversation between Jesus and Nicodemus in John 3:1-21 contains the main elements of what Christian faith intends by the term "regeneration" and the equivalent terms "new birth" and "born again." Jesus tells Nicodemus, "No one can see the kingdom of God unless he is born again [or 'born from above,' a better translation of the Greek]" (John 3:3). The Teacher is instructing Nicodemus that a person's moral goodness and righteous works are insufficient qualifications for the kingdom of God. Instead, a radical inward change is needed, a change so transforming that it can be described only as being "born again."

This metaphor of "new birth" to describe one's entrance into the Christian life emphasizes the *decisiveness* of this radical change. The regenerate person has ceased to be the person who once lived; the old life is over, and a new life has begun (Col. 3:9-10; 2 Cor. 5:17).

The "new birth" image also portrays the *one-sidedness* of this work of grace. It is altogether God's *doing*. In the physical realm, human beings do not bring about their own procreation and birth. Likewise, in the spiritual realm, they cannot give new birth to themselves. New birth is "from above." It is the work of the divine Spirit.

When Nicodemus finds it difficult to understand what it means to be born again, Jesus resorts to an illustration about the blowing wind. He says to the puzzled Pharisee, "The wind blows wherever it pleases. You hear its sound, but you cannot tell where it comes from or where it is going. So it is with everyone born of the Spirit" (John 3:8).

William Temple interprets Jesus as saying: "Don't ask for credentials. Don't wait till you know the source of the wind before you let it refresh you, or its destination before you spread sail to it. It offers what you need; trust yourself to it" (*Readings in St. John's Gospel,* 46). We can best understand the puzzlement of Nicodemus if we forget that we are modern people and imagine ourselves living in the ancient Near East. Today we have meteorologists who can tell, with some degree of accuracy, where the wind comes from and where it will go. But for the ancients, the wind was a mysterious force. They could see its effects but did not know its source or its destination.

Even for us moderns, the wind is still not without mystery. The breeze fans our foreheads, plays in the trees above, whispers in the grass below. It is an invisible current, and all our observation with the naked eye cannot tell where that current began and where it will cease. "So it is with everyone born of the Spirit," says the Master. The process is mysterious.

A hungering seeker turns his face toward heaven, receiving a divine power within. He or she is alive unto God, knowing Him, loving Him, bent upon pleasing Him. But this individual knows he or she did not originate this condition, knows he or she did not with mere human effort give birth to this new abundant life. Perhaps in some hour of mercy this person was convinced and enabled to place his or her trust in God. But he or she does not know how long the Spirit had been preparing him or her for that glad hour. This individual may know when he or she became aware that the wind of the Spirit was moving on his or her own spirit. But he or she does not know whence and how the Spirit came on its pursuing path or how this Holy Wind could blow the debris from his or her house of clay until it could become the temple of the Holy Spirit. This person knows that a Wind passed through the windows of his or her soul, not knowing how it came or where it was going.

Except for this: "The path of the righteous is like the first gleam of dawn, shining ever brighter till the full light of day" (Prov. 4:18).

And this: "What we will be has not yet been made known. But we know that when he appears, we shall be like him" (1 John 3:2).

─────────

See also

Conversion
Justification
Adoption

ADOPTION

doption is one of the three major metaphors used in the New Testament to describe what it means to be a Christian (the others being justification and regeneration).

While John and Peter favor the metaphor of regeneration to portray the beginning of the Christian life, the idea of adoption is largely Paul's idea, found only in Gal. 4:5; Rom. 8:15, 23; 9:4, and Eph. 1:5. The apostle chose a legal image (along with that of justification, which is also a legal concept), doubtless due to his firsthand knowledge of the world of Roman law. However, as noted in the essay on conversion, adoption is also a 'familial" term, conveying the idea of being brought into a new family with all its privileges.

The term for "adoption" is not found in the Old Testament, but Israel was conscious of having been chosen by God as His "son" (Hos. 11:1: Isa. 1:2; Jer. 3:19). The heathen nations surrounding Israel believed themselves to have descended from the gods. Since Israel had no such myth of descent, adoption was a fitting category to describe their relation to God as His chosen people, as well as of Israel's deliverance from Egyptian slavery, as Paul indicates in Rom. 9:4.

Furthermore, the kings succeeding David were called God's "son." The statement in Ps. 2:7, "You are my Son," was probably used in ceremonies in which each successive Davidic ruler was enthroned. These ideas laid the basis for the later New Testament use of the adoption metaphor.

The reason for our adoption is God's unconditional love in which "he predestined us to be adopted as his sons through Jesus Christ, in accordance with his pleasure and will" (Eph. 1:5). Adoption is the gift of divine grace. We are not adopted because of any merit on our part, but solely on the basis of God's loving will acting through Christ.

Paul connects adoption with the Holy Spirit. Those who are "led by the Spirit" are children of God. In Gal. 4:1-3, the law is described as enslaving the heirs until the time determined by the father. But there is a shift in verse 4 to the adoption image in which one who was a slave becomes an adopted child and thus an heir. This former slave, through the power of the Holy Spirit, now can use the address "*Abba*, Father" (v. 6).

"Abba" was a word in the Aramaic language—the language spoken in Bible lands at the time of Jesus. Not easily translatable, this word is followed in the text by the Greek term for "father," helping to establish its meaning. But "father" in most English contexts is more formal than "abba" was in Aramaic. Closer to its meaning would perhaps be "papa" or "daddy." It was an intimate, loving term a Jewish child would use to address his or her father. For that reason, it was not a word that would normally be used to address God, the one whose thoughts are higher than our thoughts and whose ways are higher than our ways (Isa. 55:8-9).

But Jesus used this very word to address God! In Gethsemane He prayed, "Abba. . . . Take this cup from me. Yet not what I will, but what you will" (Mark 14:36). We might think that Jesus, being who He was, had the right to address God in such intimate terms, while the rest of us do not. But the apostle Paul tells us that because the Holy Spirit (the same Holy Spirit who was in Jesus) dwells in us, we, too, like Jesus, can call God our "Abba." Since we're His children by adoption, we're heirs of God and co-heirs with Christ (Rom. 8:15-17).

However, adoption is not only a description of one aspect of our conversion to Christ in our past. It also has a future aspect, for it includes the redemption of the body. The legal declaration has been made. The Spirit has been given as a down payment. But the full consummation of our adoption lies beyond this present existence, where "we wait for adoption, the redemption of our bodies" (Rom. 8:23). Our adoption is something we possess now and also something for which we hope. It is "already, but not yet."

Adoption is the apex of our conversion to Christ. In justification our guilt is removed. In regeneration we are given new life. In adoption we are given, through the Spirit dwelling in us, the intimate privilege of saying "Abba" to the God whose heirs we are.

See also
   Conversion
   Justification
   Regeneration

ASSURANCE

C an we know for sure that we are saved? Answering that question is what the doctrine of *assurance* is all about. Wesleyan theology has developed that doctrine in a way that has helped strengthen the faith of countless believers.

In Catholicism, assurance is often temporary. After making confession and receiving absolution from the priest, one has great assurance. But in ensuing days as more sins accumulate, assurance diminishes until the next absolution.

In strictly traditional Calvinism, with its doctrine of unconditional election, those whom God has eternally elected to salvation have absolute assurance. But there's a hitch: in this life, not even the devout Calvinist can be completely certain that or she is among the elect. To decide it on the basis of morality, good works, or feelings would be to put his or her trust in self instead of God. According to this idea, only when a person lands safely in heaven will that person know for sure that he or she was elected.

So both Catholicism and Calvinism fall short in the kind of assurance they offer. By contrast, John Wesley taught that one who was saved could know it now, with certainty.

In 1735 Wesley sailed to North America to preach to the Indians in Georgia "in the hopes," he said, "of saving my own soul." After more than two years of failure and disappointment, he returned to England, writing in his journal, "I want that faith which none can have without knowing that he hath it" (*Works*, 1:77).

Back in London, on May 24, 1738, Wesley attended a meeting on Aldersgate Street, where, he tells us, "About a quarter before nine . . . I felt my heart strangely warmed. I felt I did trust in Christ, Christ alone for salvation: And an assurance was given me, that he had taken away *my* sins, even *mine*, and saved *me* from the law of sin and death" (*Works*, 1:103).

Later, Wesley developed his understanding of the Spirit's witness, dividing it into two parts—the *direct witness* and the *indirect witness*.

The direct witness is "an inward impression on the soul, whereby the Spirit of God directly witnesses to my spirit, that I am a child of God; that Jesus Christ hath loved me and given Himself for me; and that all my sins are blotted out, and I, even I, am reconciled to God" (*Works*, 5:115).

The direct witness, then, is something inward and subjective. The indirect witness is outward, relating to the evidence of a change in one's life. It involves the awareness of a change from darkness to light, a life producing the fruit of the Spirit and a love for God that motivates one to keep His commandments.

It's important to keep these two in balance. One should not rely solely on the direct witness. This would lead to a subjective reliance on inner feeling. Neither should one rely solely on the indirect witness, which would result in Phariseeism, or works righteousness. Both are important, and they must compliment each other.

At first Wesley thought every believer would always have assurance. But he came to see that a sense of having received forgiveness could not be a condition of receiving it. One might be justified without at first enjoying assurance, although the believed assurance would follow. He saw that even the best of Christians are sometimes buffeted with doubts. Late in his ministry he wrote in a letter to Melville Horne, "When fifty years ago my brother Charles and I, in the simplicity of our hearts, told the good people of England that unless they *knew* their sins were forgiven, they were under the wrath and curse of God, I marvel, they did not stone us!" (*The Standard Sermons of John Wesley*, 1:82n.).

The important thing is to place our trust in God's justifying grace regardless of feelings. It's our further privilege to know, by the Holy Spirit's witness, that we're justified. But *how* we know it we could probably never explain, at least not to one who doesn't have it.

But this we believe: assurance is not something that depends on priestly absolution. It is the Holy Spirit who, both directly and indirectly, "bears witness with our spirit that we are children of God" (Rom. 8:16). Nor is it something we receive for certain only after we die; it is a gift for this present life.

See also
Adoption
Conversion

HOLINESS

The word "holiness" describes the essential nature of God. One of the great Christian hymns addresses the deity as "Holy, holy, holy! Lord God Almighty!" and one of its lines is "only Thou are holy—there is none beside Thee."

To say that God is holy is simply to say that God is God. Holiness means separation. "I am God, and there is none like Me" (Isa. 46:9). To be holy means basically to be "set apart." It means to be "different." God is different from all created things in terms of His transcendence, majesty, moral perfection, and sovereign love. That God is holy means He is different from everything that is not God.

In describing God as the "Holy One," the Bible declares the majesty, glory, sovereignty, and unfathomable mystery that mark the divine being. Thus, holiness belongs to the very definition of God. Even love, which is the center of the Christian concept of God, must be seen against the background of His holiness.

God alone is holy. His holiness is unique to Him and belongs to no other being except as He imparts it. It points to the inscrutable mystery and otherness of God, to the separation between the Creator and the creaturely.

We begin to see the richness of the biblical understanding of God's holiness in Exod. 3:5. The ground on which Moses stands is holy, because God is there. Only God and that which is associated with Him can be called holy. Holiness is inseparable from God's presence.

Following Moses' encounter with God at the burning bush, many things are called holy in the Old Testament. For instance, there are holy places, holy vessels, holy oil, holy seasons, and holy people. But all these are called holy for one reason only—they stand in a particular relation to the holy God. They are substantially the same as other places, vessels, oil, seasons, and people that are *not* called holy. The difference is that some are set apart for God and some are not. Thus, when any of God's creations, including human beings, are said to be holy, it means they are set apart for God's exclusive use.

Insofar as holiness may be ascribed to beings other than God, it is a derivative of God's holiness and has its origin in Him. This means that holiness is first and foremost a *religious* concept and not a moral or ethical one. In other words, its primary focus is *vertical* rather than *horizontal*. But "holiness," as it is progressively revealed in the Bible, takes on a secondary and consequential meaning that is moral and ethical (this is, horizontal), affecting all our relations with other people and with the created order. This is because God's holiness and His love are always related. The same holy love that redeems also demands that the redeemed be like Him. Fellowship with the Holy God can be established only on the basis of holiness, for "it is written: Be holy, because I am holy" (1 Pet. 1:16).

The first commandment defines what it means for a person to be holy: "You shall have no other gods before me" (Exod. 20:3). One who is holy is one who has no other gods.

Although the holiness of God, a central theme of the Old Testament, is assumed in the New Testament, the latter places the emphasis on Jesus Christ. Holiness now is defined by Jesus Christ and who He is. Jesus is the "Holy One of God" (Mark 1:24; Luke 4:34; John 6:69). His Incarnation and Atonement were for the purpose of providing a way for unholy people to be made holy and live in fellowship with a holy God (Heb. 12:14; 13:12). Thus, the term basically applied to God in the Old Testament is now seen as God's *provision* (Col. 1:22), God's *will* (1 Thess. 4:3-7), and God's *requirement* (Heb. 12:14; Rev. 22:11) for every believer.

Jesus is the very embodiment of holiness. Therefore holiness is simply Christlikeness, made possible only by divine grace. One's holiness is not to be ascertained on the basis of legalism, emotionalism, or any other criteria that we, in our humanity, are prone to impose. The only criterion is Christ. God is a Christlike God, and believers are called to be Christlike. The Living God who is Holy Love calls us to holy living and loving as Jesus the Holy One lived and loved.

See also
   Sanctification
   Perfection

SANCTIFICATION

S anctification is a precious word to people in the Wesleyan-Holiness tradition. It is also perhaps also the most misunderstood, due to the fact that in this tradition the word is used in several senses, each sense depicting an important aspect of salvation.

In its broadest sense, sanctification is the lifelong process by which Christians become the "saints" they were called to be (1 Cor. 1:2, KJV; Eph. 1:1), "perfecting holiness out of reverence for God" (2 Cor. 7:1). It is the process of moving step by step, by grace, toward our destiny. And what is our destiny? It is defined by the *image Dei* (image of God) in which we were created (Gen. 1:27). In our sin we turned away from our destiny. The "image" that is our destiny is now defined by Jesus Christ, who is "the image of the invisible God" (Col. 1:15), and "the radiance of God's glory and the exact representation of his being" (Heb. 1:3). Into that same image we "are being transformed" (2 Cor. 3:18). In short, our destiny is "to be conformed to the likeness of his Son" (Rom. 8:29).

From its human side, sanctification basically means a commitment toward Christlikeness. This commitment has been called "consecration." It is not a Christlikeness that can be attained by exerting human strength, but one that is the gift of grace and to which we are to be continually open. "Now we are children of God, and what we will be has not yet been made known. But we know that when he appears, we shall be like him" (1 John 3:2).

In this total process of sanctification are various submeanings to the word. Wesleyans hold that sanctification is both gradual and instantaneous. Regarding salvation, which he said consisted of "two grand branches, justification and sanctification," Wesley wrote,

> All experience, as well as Scripture, show this salvation to be both instantaneous and gradual. It begins the moment we are justified, in the holy, humble, gentle, patient love of God and man. It gradually increases from that moment . . . till, in another instant, the heart is cleansed from all sin, and filled with pure love to God and man. But even that love increases more and more, till "we grow up in all things into Him that is our Head;"

till we attain "the measure of the stature of the fulness of Christ" (*Works*, 6:509).

Let us analyze that statement, for it contains the various senses in which Wesleyans use the term "sanctification." That which "begins the moment we are justified" is often called *initial sanctification*, which is one aspect of the conversion experience.

This sanctification, beginning at conversion, "gradually increases from that moment" and may be called *gradual* sanctification.

"Till, in another instant, the heart is cleansed from all sin, and filled with pure love to God and man." This is called *entire sanctification* and is the most distinctive aspect of the Wesleyan understanding of holiness. All historic Christian churches believe in sanctification, but some deny the possibility of *entire* sanctification in this life.

"But even that love increases more and more." Both before and after the instantaneous work of entire sanctification, the gradual work of sanctification goes on. Sanctification is never a "static state" that "does not admit of a continual increase" (*Works*, 6:5). Some Holiness writers have claimed that sanctification is always instantaneous and never gradual. They claim that there is the "instant" of *initial* sanctification and another "instant" of *entire* sanctification, and that everything before, between, and following those instants is simply "growth in grace." But to attempt to define "growth in grace" as anything other than gradual or progressive sanctification seems like a hairsplitting exercise in futility. It's difficult, if not impossible, to clearly show the difference. It's better to stick with the original Wesleyan understanding that sanctification is *both* instantaneous *and* gradual. Of course, in Wesleyanism, *entire* sanctification is instantaneous (there may come an instant when, in the words of Wesley quoted above, "the heart is cleansed from all sin"), but *sanctification* in its broadest meaning is both/and.

We may also speak of *final* sanctification, occurring at the resurrection, when scars from sin will be forever healed. The point is that there are several senses in which Wesleyans use the term "sanctification." To understand these is to be a better-informed Christian in the Wesleyan tradition.

See also
Holiness
Perfection

PERFECTION

Perfection. What a scary word! "So who's perfect?" we ask when we slip up and make some goofy mistake.

Perfection! When used in a religious context, the word frightens some Christians and discourages many others. It seems so absolute. So impossible.

But the word found in the Scriptures is not so impossible. Unfortunately, our modern use of the word is closely associated with flawlessness, like a perfectly cut diamond in the jewelry store window with its facets sparkling in the light. It is often understood as the last state in a progression. (It is possible that Luke perceived such a possible connotation of the word used by Matthew in 5:48, and uses instead the word "merciful" in Luke 6:36.)

To be perfect as our heavenly Father is perfect (Matt. 5:48) is to be wholly turned, with the whole will and being, to God, as He is turned to us. It is the response of obedience carried out in faith. It is the call to be pure in heart, and to will one thing. The command falls within a *religious* situation, not simply a moral situation of improving our conduct by strenuous effort.

"Perfect" in the Bible does not have a legalistic background. Nor does it have a pietist authority as though perfection could be achieved by human effort in the "imitation of Christ." It belongs in the category of *grace*. "Be perfect" is the command of God that can call forth from our hearts only one response, that of faith.

Our obedience in faith is not the beginning of some vague progress in climbing up a ladder of moral achievement. It is the acceptance of grace, which is always whole, complete, perfect. In the strength of this encounter we live our lives. "Perfect" belongs only to God. It comes to us through our contact with Him, not as an achievement, but as a *gift*. All that God is and has is perfect and whole, never partial. Our share in this kind of wholeness is determined by the veracity of our relation to Him.

John Wesley preached "Christian perfection" (not the same thing as "sinless perfection"), and what he meant by it was so often misunderstood that on at least one occasion he considered dropping the term. He said his opponents continually thrust it on him by asking what he meant by it. But in spite of this claim, Wesley did frequently use the term in his preaching and writings. The reason was that it was a Scriptural term, and Wesley was passionately attached to the language of Scripture. He claimed that no one could in good conscience object to such a scriptural term "unless we would send the Holy Ghost to school and teach Him to speak who made the tongue" (*Letters*, 4:212).

Nevertheless, instead of "Christian perfection," Wesley preferred the term "perfect love." In his proclamation of Christian perfection, the stress always fell on love, "love filling the heart, and governing all the words and actions" (*Works*, 11:401).

This love of which Wesley spoke was not mere sentiment, not mere feeling or emotion. It was love as an attitude, a state of mind, and a set will. This love was robust, objective, and sometimes stern. He did not preach love as a mystical and emotional relation to Christ, as of a bride to her husband. He disliked such doctrines, thinking them smudged with sentimentality and leading to erotic excess.

Love was, to Wesley, the essence of perfection, and to attempt to define it in any other category was to go astray. "Let this love be attained, by whatever means," he said, "and I am content; I desire no more. All is well, if we love the Lord our God with all our heart, and our neighbour as ourselves" (*Letters*, 2:75).

So who's perfect? Only those who are perfectly turned toward God, in the spirit of the psalmist, who could pray, "Search me, O God, and know my heart; test me and know my anxious thoughts. See if there is any offensive way in me, and lead me in the way everlasting" (Ps. 139:23-24). Only those who are perfectly turned toward their needful neighbor in love and compassion. Only those who know they are not flawless, but are maturing. Only those who can come to God in complete faith, in the utter dearth of feelings, with the weight of failures, neglects, and imperfections pressing heavily on their hearts, and say to Him, "You are my refuge."

See also
   Holiness
   Sanctification

TEMPTATION

T he Epistle to the Hebrews declares that Jesus the Son of God "has been tempted in every way, just as we are" (4:15). If we can understand this declaration, we will understand our own temptations.

Our Lord's temptation followed immediately after the high point of His baptism and the Father's voice saying, "This is my Son, whom I love" (Matt. 3:17). Following on the heels of that great experience, "Jesus was led by the Spirit into the desert to be tempted by the devil" (4:1). Our own worst temptations often follow our "mountaintop" experiences. With Jesus it was no different.

Matt. 4:1-11 tells us how Jesus was tempted "in every way"— three ways, to be exact. Our own temptations will usually *in principle* fall into one of these three categories:

First, He was tempted to turn stones into bread (Matt. 4:3). We may think that is so far removed from our own temptations as to be irrelevant. But the issue facing Jesus is this: shall I satisfy a legitimate hunger now, placing a physical need above a spiritual one, or shall I postpone satisfaction until it can be fulfilled in the proper way and at the proper time? Deferred satisfaction is something our hedonistic age doesn't like to consider. There are many ways in which this principle may encroach upon us. Take just one example, that of premarital or extramarital sex. The issue here is identical to the issue in our Lord's temptation to turn stones into bread—whether to satisfy a legitimate God-given hunger in an illegitimate way, or to postpone satisfaction until it can be fulfilled according to God's design.

Second, Jesus was tempted to do something spectacular (leap from a Temple tower unharmed) to gain the applause and allegiance of the crowd (Matt. 4:5-6). People were longing for a leader who could deliver them from Roman bondage. Many would-be messiahs had tried to capitalize on this longing. Jesus was tempted to take the easy road to Messiahship. The lure of the sensational has drawn many a Christian off the straight-and-narrow path. Fallible humans can easily be dazzled into following a wonder-working leader.

Third, Jesus was tempted to compromise His principles by bowing down and worshiping Satan. He could have "all the kingdoms of the world" (v. 8) if He would just shade the truth a little, shave His demands a little, offer people "cheap grace," and make it easier for people to be His followers. If Christ could be thus tempted, so can every Christian. And so can the Church. We don't have to join a Satanist cult to be Satan-worshipers. We need only to adopt his methods.

In Christ's temptations, several facts stand out:

1. The Father had said, "This is my Son" (Matt. 3:17). Now Satan says, *"If* you are the Son of God . . ." (Matt. 4:3, 6), planting a doubt in Jesus' mind regarding His true identity.

2. The actions that Satan suggested were not obviously evil in themselves. Eating when one is hungry, seeking to win people to God's cause, and desiring to claim the "kingdoms of the world" for God are not evil on their face. We would seldom be tempted if the actions suggested to us were always clearly and unquestionably wrong. Satan does not come to us with horns and a forked tail, clad in a red suit and wielding a pitchfork! Rather, he cleverly disguises himself as "an angel of light" (2 Cor. 11:14).

3. Our Lord's temptations were *real.* A few still teach the ancient Apollinarian heresy, that it was impossible for Jesus to have yielded to temptation. But Heb. 4:15 says He was tempted "just as we are," and certainly it is possible for us to yield. There is no moral value in the sinlessness of one who could not sin. Rocks cannot sin—moral beings can.

4. Our Lord's temptation to take the easy road did not end following the event recorded in Matt. 4:11 but was a continual struggle, as seen in the conversation at Caesarea Philippi (Matt. 16:23) and in the prayer in Gethsemane (Matt. 26:36-45).

5. Jesus defeated Satan by relying on the Word of God, quoting from Deuteronomy (Matt. 4:4, 7, 10). He who was "tempted in every way, just as we are" knew His weaponry. The power of God's Word was stronger than Satan. Seeing he was defeated, Satan departed. In times of temptation we, too, can defeat Satan with "the sword of the Spirit, which is the word of God" (Eph. 6:17).

See also
   Sin
   Satan

MYSTERY

I love a mystery. On my bookshelves are all the Sherlock Holmes stories, and I have read many of them several times. As a young man, I got hooked on the "whodunits" of Agatha Christie and Erle Stanley Gardner, and I have enjoyed mystery stories ever since. When I search for something of interest in the vast wasteland of television, the British *Mystery* series on public television often claims my attention. Reading or listening to a mystery story, I can become totally absorbed in trying to anticipate the ending before I get to it. I really do love a mystery.

And so did Paul! The word "mystery" (*mysterion* in Greek) occurs many times in his epistles. But there was only one that he really cared about, and he repeated it over and over again.

For the apostle, a mystery meant something hidden in God's eternal and inscrutable will, which we could not discover by our human ingenuity and deductive powers. That's the bad news. But the good news is this: *The mystery has been revealed to believers through Jesus Christ* (see Rom. 16:25-26; 1 Cor. 2:7-10; Eph. 1:9; 3:9; Col. 1:26). Paul saw Christ as the great demystifier, a solver of mysteries rather than a maker of them. But it is only for the person of faith that this mystery is truly "solved."

The mystery Paul talks about is the unexplainable "depth of the riches of the wisdom and knowledge of God" (Rom. 11:33). He understood this mystery to be the ineffable way in which the hidden purpose of God is made known in Christ (Eph. 1:9; 3:4-5; Col. 2:2; 4:3), in the *gospel* (Eph. 6:19), through the *Church* (Eph. 3:9-10), and in individual *believers* (Col. 1:26).

Paul's expression of Christ as a *mysterion* disclosed by God to the believer is a profound and consistent development of the word of Jesus, "To you it has been given to know the mystery of the kingdom of God" (Mark 4:11, NKJV). Redemption is a mystery we cannot solve on our own. It "has been given." God himself has let the secret out! Ahead of time! Before we reach the end!

One of the ways we receive the mystery is through the sacraments of the Church. In the writings of the Early Church fathers in the West, the Greek *mysterion* was usually translated by the Latin *sacramentum*, from which we get our word "sacrament." Of course, *mysterion* is not used in the New Testament to denote those specific actions commanded by Christ, which the Church came to call "sacraments." But Paul's *idea* of mystery nevertheless connects with the Church's understanding of sacrament, so that the meanings of the two terms correspond. To the unbeliever the sacraments are just so much meaningless human activity, but to the person of faith they become a revelation of the inner meaning of the gospel. Like Nathanael, who asked if any good could come from Nazareth, a skeptic might ask, "Can anything really significant happen to us in baptism and at the Lord's Table?" Like Philip, the believer replies, "Come and see" (John 1:46). What is Christ doing for us in the sacraments? They who know are those who love the mystery!

In most mysteries, it's only at the end of the story that everything falls into place. But in the mystery of redemption, the ending is revealed right in the middle of the story. That is, in the midst of human history, Christ came. And when we read history from the middle, there are no surprise endings. Christ is the "whodunit" in this great mystery that is the gospel story. He came in human flesh. He died for our transgressions. He was raised from the dead. He was exalted to God's right hand. And He will come again.

To us who await His coming, the apostle John has a message: "Dear friends, now we are children of God, and what we will be has not yet been made known. But we know that when he appears, we shall be like him, for we shall see him as he is" (1 John 3:2).

That is good news! I love a mystery.

─────

See also
   God
   Creation
   Incarnation

PREDESTINATION

A man who had just received his private pilot's license invited his friend to go for a plane ride. His friend refused, saying he was afraid to get that high off the ground. Being unable to convince the man that flying was safer than riding in a car, he said, "I thought you believed in predestination and that nobody can die until his time comes."

"I do," replied his friend.

"Then if you know you cannot die until your time comes, what's the problem?" asked the pilot.

"Well," his friend explained, "what if we get up in the air and *your* time comes?"

This humorous story illustrates the difficulties that may arise from a wrong understanding of predestination. But predestination *is* a biblical doctrine. The problem is that some theological traditions have distorted the doctrine into a deterministic idea that leaves no room for human freedom, teaching that God has ordered all things according to His inscrutable will and therefore causes every detail that happens. This includes the notion that from all eternity some people are predestined to be saved and some predestined to be damned, and that nothing we do can alter either destiny.

What, then, does the Bible mean by predestination? In short, it means that our salvation is God's eternal purpose for everyone. We are all "predestined to be conformed to the likeness of his Son" (Rom. 8:29). Thus, we are predestined for holy living, "for he chose us in him before the creation of the world to be holy and blameless in his sight" (Eph. 1:4). But the Bible also teaches that we have freedom to accept or reject the destiny God has planned for us. When we reject salvation, we are spurning that which has been God's saving purpose for us since the very beginning. Such saving purpose is "to the praise of his glorious grace which he has freely given us in the One he loves" (Eph. 1:6).

In Flannery O'Conner's short story "The River," an uneducated preacher, self-styled healer, and baptizer named Bevel Summers, standing knee-deep in water at the river's edge, snatches a four-year-old boy from his babysitter on the bank and, before the child knows what's happening, immerses him in the water. He then says to the dripping and startled boy, "You count now; you didn't even count before." As the story unfolds, O'Conner shows how this mis-guided understanding—both of baptism and of God—soon brings about the boy's self-destruction.

No, we do not baptize or dedicate children because of a faulty belief that they don't count unless we do so. We do it because they *do* count—already—with God. The idea of predestination tells us that we all count, that God loves us from all eternity and has pro-vided a way of salvation for us, which cost Him the death of His only begotten Son.

But what about human freedom? Does our vote count? How do we harmonize these two biblical truths: (1) We are admonished to seek the Lord and choose the way of salvation (Isa. 55:6), and (2) We are saved by God's grace and not by anything we do (Eph. 2:8-9)? Although these truths may appear to be in conflict, in reality they are not. They are two facets of the same shining reality. When we approach the door of salvation, we find inscribed on the outside of the door, as it were, the words "Choose you this day whom you will serve." But when we freely exercise saving faith, open the door, and enter into salvation, we can turn around and find inscribed on the inside of the door the words "You have not chosen me, but I have chosen you."

Several years ago Reformed theologian Hendrikus Berkhof of the Netherlands visited my theology class at Nazarene Theological Seminary, where I invited him to speak. After talking awhile, he opened the floor for questions. One student asked him if he be-lieved in predestination. "Yes, I do," he replied, "but we Calvinists have distorted that doctrine by turning it into a tight logical deter-ministic system. Its real purpose is religious and not philosophical. It was really meant as a great devotional truth. It simply means this: When we get to the end of the journey, we will have to say it was God who brought us all the way."

We Wesleyans believe that too!

━━━━━

See also
  Providence

CHURCH

Being a Christian is more than a merely *individual* affair. "Christianity is essentially a social religion," said John Wesley, "and . . . to turn it into a solitary religion, is indeed to destroy it" (Wesley, *Works*, 5:296).

Pentecost was a *corporate* affair. When the disciples were assembled in the Upper Room, the Holy Spirit came to rest "on each of them" (Acts 2:3, NRSV), but it was only when "they were all together in one place" (Acts 2:1, NRSV). Each person individually experienced the Holy Spirit, but only as all of them were knit together in a common quest and a common obedience (Luke 24:49).

At the close of his Pentecost sermon, Peter states that the same Holy Spirit will be bestowed on those who repent and are baptized. Baptism, as God's covenant sign, marks the bestowal of the Spirit, and it is the Spirit who thus creates and constitutes the Church.

One of the most vivid metaphors of the Church in the New Testament is Paul's reference to it as "the Body of Christ." When this metaphor is coupled with the correlative image of Christ as "the head of the body" (Col. 1:18), a striking picture of the Church emerges. Each individual Christian is a part ("member") of Christ's Body, living in harmony with the other parts, and under the control of the Head!

These parts all come together and find their meaning in the living fellowship of the Church into which we're initiated by baptism. Wesley said, "By baptism we are admitted into the Church, and consequently made members of Christ, its Head" (Wesley, *Works*, 10:191).

The Nicene Creed declares that baptism is no mere appendage, but an integral element of our Christian faith. It says in part,

> I believe in one holy catholic and apostolic church.
> I acknowledge one baptism for the remission of sins.

The gospel is not a system of timeless ideas but is rooted in the soil of a particular history where the Word was made flesh. Therefore, our appropriation of the gospel is not an abstract, inward, invisible acceptance, but is ever expressed in a given, historical, visible outward sign so that the Word may become flesh in our own experience. That sign is baptism. To dispense with the sign, the Creed seems to tell us, would be to scorn the thing signified. Of course, the inward grace may exist without the outward sign, but the mainstream of Christianity has held that the inward grace is best appropriated when the outward sign is given its proper place.

In its affirmation of "one baptism," the Nicene Creed is faithful to the New Testament, especially to the Epistle to the Ephesians, that eloquent and exultant description of the majesty of our Christian faith. In a beautiful passage there, the apostle Paul sums up the whole magnitude of Christian experience. He has already shown how God's gracious love has bridged the chasm of sin and overcome deep divisions within humanity to create a redemptive order of fellowship in Christ. Now he exhorts his readers to maintain the unity of the Spirit that God's love has created. Such unity is at the very heart of Christian reality: "There is one body and one Spirit—just as you were called to one hope when you were called—one Lord, one faith, one baptism; one God and Father of all, who is over all and through all and in all" (Eph. 4:4-6).

There is one body! "I believe in one holy catholic and apostolic Church." The unity of the Church is often obscured by the fragmentation of a divided Christendom. Yet the Church remains one. There are many members but one body, and "to each one of us grace has been given as Christ apportioned it" (Eph. 4:7). The Church, which is Christ's Body, is not to be built out of the denominational structures, but *into* them! Baptism expresses our initiation into this one Body. As divergent as our several denominational traditions may be, it is a tremendous truth that one baptismal formula gathers us all together as one body—"in the name of the Father and of the Son and of the Holy Spirit." Amen.

━━━━━━

See also
   Worship
   Sacraments
   Baptism
   Eucharist

WORSHIP

I don't go to church anymore," said the talkative man seated next to me on Delta flight 204 when he learned I was on my way to speak about worship and sacraments at a district seminar for pastors. I thought I detected a note of sadness in his voice.

"Why did you stop?" I asked.

"Well," he replied, "I tried several different churches and, to be perfectly frank, I just don't get anything out of it."

"Well, to be perfectly frank," I replied, "who said you were supposed to?"

Somewhat taken aback, he stammered, "Uh—how's that again?" So I tried to explain that the main purpose of church attendance is not to "get something out of it" but to worship and glorify God. The question is not what I can get out of church, but what God gets out of it when I deliberately stay home, or even when I'm present and yet fail to give myself over to His worship and praise. To paraphrase a line from an oft-quoted presidential inaugural speech of a few decades ago, "Ask not what your God can do for you, but ask what you can do for your God."

Oh, I know we can and should "get something" out of church. And I know that petition is part of the prayer Jesus taught us to pray. There's nothing wrong with asking for our daily bread or any other genuine need. But true worshipers have learned that the "getting" best comes as a by-product of the "giving."

The Westminster Shorter Catechism had it right in its very first question: "What is the chief end of man?" Answer: "The chief end of man is to glorify God, and to enjoy him forever." Now that's really "getting something out of it"—enjoying God forever! But the order is important—the *getting* follows the *glorifying*.

The top priority of Christ's Church is worship. Not missions, not evangelism, not church growth. (I can smell the smoke, but please don't burn me at the stake just yet.) Those concerns *are* important, but their importance is *secondary*, albeit very near the top and just below it. Our *primary* concern as Christians should be the

81

worship of God. Take care of that, and the other priorities will become even more urgent as well as more authentic.

We often hear (and read) that the Church's chief mandate is the Great Commission. I beg to differ just a little. Our chief mandate is the Great *Commandment*: "Love the Lord your God with all your heart and with all your soul and with all your mind and with all your strength" (Mark 12:30). Placing the Great *Commission* ahead of the Great *Commandment* will likely, in the long run, be the great *disillusionment*.

A pastor's chief assignment is to lead the people in the worship of God. The conversation with my seat companion on the plane revealed that he was the product of this present relativistic, hedonistic, pragmatic, utilitarian, consumer-oriented age. He had sat under pastors who were so busy trying to be useful in building the Kingdom that they had become excessively utilitarian.

But it works both ways. Many pastors have been molded to a great extent by their people's *expectations* of them—expectations that may likewise have replaced the Church's primary mandate with a secondary one. But God, in His unencumbered holiness, refuses to be useful! His ministries are not finally utilitarian.

When Satan tempted Jesus to be pragmatic and utilitarian, promising that He would "get something out of it"—even all the kingdoms of the world—our Lord responded, "It is written, 'Worship the Lord your God, and serve him only'" (Matt. 4:10, NRSV).

The debate in recent years about the type of worship that best attracts people, the so-called worship wars between traditional and contemporary styles of worship, seems to miss the main point. The question itself is phrased in pragmatic terms: "What works best?"

People simply yearn, deep in their hearts, to hear the note of eternity in the sanctuary. Let that note be sounded! Let God be glorified! Let Christ be exalted! And who knows? We just might "get something out of it" after all!

See also
Church
Liturgy
Sacraments
Play

LITURGY

The word "liturgy" comes from the Greek word *leitourgia*, which in turn comes from *leitos* (public) and *ergon* (work). It thus means "the people's work." This does not refer to the work one does to make a living, but to the actions performed in the context of worship. Liturgy includes the ceremonial rites, rituals, and exercises performed by the worshiping congregation in a church service. In some denominational contexts—particularly those churches commonly perceived as the more "liturgical' ones—it refers to the official, authorized forms and rituals of public, corporate worship and administration of the sacraments.

But all churches have liturgy. Corporate worship would be practically impossible without it. Some liturgies are more elaborate than others, and the more elaborate ones get labeled "liturgical," while the simpler ones are sometimes spoken of as "nonliturgical." But liturgy is the vital and indispensable framework for worship. The "people's work" includes such actions as reading and exposition of scripture; the recitation of creeds; the singing of Psalms, hymns, and spiritual songs; common prayers; and sacraments.

All churches have liturgy. Even the early Quaker meetings in which the people sat in silence until the Spirit moved someone to speak were liturgical. The act of sitting in silent meditation was a prescribed liturgical form and often a very effective one. In evangelistic services the invitation, or altar call, is also a liturgy.

In Hellenistic culture the word is used to describe an act of public service. In the Old Testament it denotes the work of priests and Levites as they serve in the Tabernacle and the Temple. In fact, the underlying patterns of Christian liturgy were derived from Judaism, such as the sacramental actions of baptism and ceremonial feasts, the use of Psalms, rituals of confession of sin, prayers of intercession and dedication, and thanksgivings and blessings. As such patterns became transfused with specifically Christian beliefs about the Person and saving work of Christ, these Jewish forms of liturgy were gradually developed and elaborated by the Church into certain forms of worship that became classic in later centuries.

In the New Testament, as in the Old, the word denotes service in the Temple (Luke 1:23; Heb. 9:21). In Acts 13:2 it refers to worship. In the works of the early church fathers it refers to the whole service of God, particularly the activities of the pastoral office. Later, the term became more restricted, referring largely to the Lord's Supper.

The past several decades have seen a revival of interest in liturgy. This is doubtless a reaction against the excessive individualism that has characterized Western society since the close of the Middle Ages. Liturgy is in principle an instrument of group participation and responsibility. It does not depend upon individual gifts of inspiration or leadership, however valuable these may be when available. At its best, liturgical worship provides the poorest member of the congregation with the full richness of faith and devotion and at the same time provides an opportunity for the humblest member to make a maximum contribution to the community of the faithful.

Ideally, liturgy should be both *objective* and *subjective*, combining adoration and praise of the triune God with the experience of the grace, forgiveness, and blessing of God through the Holy Spirit. It is an expression to God of the attitudes and aspirations of the worshiper, and a vehicle for uniting the congregation in worship.

Ironically, people brought up in so-called nonliturgical churches sometimes have the impression that liturgy makes the worshiper merely a spectator. But at its best, liturgy does just the opposite—it makes everyone in the congregation active participants.

Liturgy is not an enemy of spiritual worship. Of course, liturgy can be cold and lifeless. Although the Holy Spirit is able to work without structured liturgy, such lack of structure is not to be sought as the ideal. Rather, the ideal is liturgy that's always open to the Spirit. The quest for spiritual reality cannot be satisfied with that which is superficial, shallow, and merely subjective. Full satisfaction comes from the Word of God—the incarnate Word, the written word of Scripture, the preached Word of sermon, and the "visible word" of sacrament. Such satisfaction will be attained to the extent that we wholeheartedly participate in liturgy—"the people's work."

━━━━━━━

See also
Worship

SACRAMENTS

Most Protestant churches believe in two "sacraments," namely baptism and the Lord's Supper. But what is a sacrament?

John Wesley defined a sacrament as "an outward sign of inward grace, and a means whereby we receive the same." Centuries earlier, in a short and almost perfect definition, Augustine referred to sacraments as "visible words." Preaching and teaching are audible words that convey a message through the hearing of the ear. But a visible word is any sign or action that conveys a message by being *done* and *seen*.

Roman Catholics believe in seven sacraments. Most Protestants affirm only the two mentioned above, mainly because in the New Testament only those two are directly related to the forgiveness of sins, which is grounded in Christ's atoning death (see Rom. 6:1-4 on baptism and Matt. 26:28 on the Lord's Supper).

The word "sacrament" is thought to have come originally from the Latin *sacramentum*, which in ancient times referred to a sum of money that both parties to a lawsuit deposited with a third party—something like putting money in "escrow," as we would say today. This foreshadowed one aspect of a Christian sacrament, especially as understood by Protestants, namely, that a sacrament involves the use of some physical element as a "sign" or "symbol."

Later *sacramentum* came to refer to the oath of allegiance taken by a Roman soldier as he promised to serve and defend the Roman Empire. This anticipated yet another element inherent in a sacrament, namely, the word of promise that accompanies the sign and without which the sign would not have its sacramental character. Taken together, these two early meanings of the Latin *sacramentum* convey two important aspects in the idea of a Christian sacrament—an action involving a physical element used as a symbol (water, bread, wine), and a word of promise accompanying the use of the symbol, namely the New Covenant promise of grace.

Thus, the English word "sacrament," deriving from the Latin *sacramentum*, came into use in the language of faith to indicate cer-

tain religious actions or events. The term was "baptized" into the
Christian vocabulary! Although the word "sacrament" is not found
in Scripture with the specific meaning assigned to it in Christian
history, it is a legitimate term for the actions the Church has found
to be practiced in Scripture and commanded by the Lord.

Sacraments are not the same as "ordinances." The latter word
denotes a religious rite that has been commanded—something we
are to *do*. "Sacrament" has a richer meaning. It denotes something
that *is done for us*. Most churches in the Wesleyan tradition consider baptism and the Lord's Supper to be sacraments, not ordinances.

What, then, do sacraments *do* for us? In keeping with most of
Christian history, John Wesley, our theological and spiritual "grandfather," classified sacraments as "means of grace," by which he
meant "outward signs, words, or actions, ordained of God . . . to be
the ordinary channels whereby he might convey . . . preventing,
justifying, or sanctifying grace" (*Works*, 5:187).

In short, sacraments convey *grace* if we come to them in faith—
grace for whatever our need may be. Our God is a *God who acts*. In
the waters of baptism, and at the table of the Lord when we receive
the bread and the cup, we become the beneficiaries of the action of
God, who imparts His grace to us here and now.

Sacraments safeguard the biblical doctrine of *creation* against
the early heresy of gnosticism, which was a dualistic theory holding
that all matter was evil. Whenever we submit to being baptized
with water (matter) and drink the fruit of the vine (matter), we are
affirming something about our *redemption*. But also—and admitted-
ly secondary to it—we are saying something about the *creation*. We
are combating all forms of dualism. We are affirming that these ma-
terial elements are a vehicle, a "residency" of divine grace. We are
saying that this physical world is essentially good. And that's what
God said about it in the beginning!

See also
> Grace
> Baptism
> Paedobaptism
> Eucharist

BAPTISM

The New Testament knows nothing of "unbaptized Christians." No such phenomenon existed in the Early Church, unless you count the repentant thief on the Cross, and he can hardly be our example, for he had no opportunity to be baptized.

A New Testament identifies Christians as those who have repented and been baptized (Acts 2:37-38), those who have been "baptized into Christ Jesus" and "buried with him through baptism into death" (Rom. 6:3-4). Therefore, if we follow the New Testament pattern, we will not neglect this holy sacrament.

This is not to say that baptism is absolutely necessary for salvation. As my grandfather used to say, "One can go down a dry sinner and come up a wet sinner!" But *faith* is necessary, and one part of faith is obedience. If Christ willed that we be baptized, as the Great Commission makes clear (Matt. 28:19), then why would any Christian wish to disobey?

Baptism marks the Christian as belonging to God. God has always marked His people. Under the old covenant, God ordained the sign of circumcision by which to mark His chosen people (Gen. 17:11). Likewise, baptism is the mark of initiation into the new covenant. In Col. 2:11-12, Paul brings the old and the new sacramental symbols together and links them with the death and resurrection of Christ. Paul declares that baptism, having replaced circumcision, is now the new *outward sign* of the *inward grace* by which the Colossian Christians had been buried and raised with Christ.

John Wesley saw baptism as the fulfillment and replacement of circumcision, and the Wesleyan-Holiness tradition has generally followed him in this. "It is," he said, "the initiatory sacrament," which is instituted in place of circumcision and which "enters us into covenant with God" (*Works* 10:188).

What is the proper *mode* of baptism—immersion, sprinkling, or pouring? Since an airtight case cannot be made from Scripture for either mode (despite many attempts to do so), most churches in the Wesleyan tradition allow baptism to be administered by sprinkling, pouring, or immersion, according to the choice of the applicant.

Each mode has its symbolic value. Immersion comes closest to symbolizing our union with Christ in His death and resurrection. Sprinkling best symbolizes the cleansing of the heart "from a guilty conscience" (Heb. 10:22) described in 9:13, 19, 21. And pouring best symbolizes the outpouring of the Holy Spirit on the Day of Pentecost.

All three modes signify aspects of the work of Christ in saving us from death to life. In fact, each mode is a window shedding light on the whole work of Jesus as Savior. Each mode of baptism participates in the meaning of the other two, so it does not matter which mode is used.

One word of caution is in order. Those who favor immersion must be careful not to denigrate the other modes. Some seem to think that the more water there is, the more valid the baptism. But baptism is a *symbolic* action. Its value is not intrinsic—it is not a particularly efficient way to take a bath! Its value lies in what it symbolizes. Size and amount are not significant factors in symbolism. If they were, there would be little value in the other sacrament, the Lord's Supper, in which the elements are provided in amounts too small to offer much physical nourishment. We humans tend to judge the value of a thing on the basis of amount and appearance, but God judges on the basis of quality and meaning. It is not the amount of water that gives baptism its value, but rather the meaning of the whole symbolic action.

Martin Luther often became so despondent that he could virtually sense Satan slithering to his side and tempting him to doubt his salvation. In such times, he could cause the devil to slink away by declaring emphatically, "I am baptized!" He knew he bore Christ's mark.

Such a declaration can be misused, causing us to rest our salvation merely on a past event. It is indeed possible for the baptized person to quench the Spirit and fall from grace. Nevertheless, there's great comfort in knowing that we've been marked as God's children by this sacrament that He has ordained. To know that we've been buried with Christ in baptism and raised to newness of life—that is life indeed!

―――――――

See also
   Sacraments
   Paedobaptism

PAEDOBAPTISM

Paedobaptism (from the Greek *paedo* for "child") is the technical term for the baptism of infants. We do not know for certain if infants were baptized in New Testament times, but there is reason for believing they were, since on a few occasions in the Book of Acts entire families were baptized upon the conversion of the father. Some of these families likely included infants or young children. But even it they did not, it would not make a case against infant baptism, because the New Testament does not trace the history of the Early Church far enough to reveal what those new converts in Acts did with the children born to them after their conversion. At least we know from history that in the early centuries, there was widespread practice of infant baptism.

Another tradition developed in the 16th century. Those known as Anabaptists insisted that baptism was for adults only, since only adults were able to understand its implications and exercise saving faith.

The doctrine of infant baptism in the Wesleyan tradition traces back through Methodist, Anglican, and classical Protestant sources to the early centuries in which it was the norm. But many in this tradition, influenced by Anabaptist or Baptist teachings, choose the alternative of infant *dedication*, postponing baptism until the child matures in understanding and can knowingly choose or reject it.

Under the old covenant, parents dedicated children to God, but there is no reference to infant dedication under the new covenant. Most churches in the Wesleyan tradition affirm infant baptism in their official statements of faith but also provide rituals for infant dedication for those who choose it.

Parents who choose to have their child *baptized* do so out of the conviction that it is not primarily *our faith* that saves us, but *God's prior grace*. God's grace precedes all human decision, and it is only secondarily and consequentially that baptism is a testimony to our human response to God. Just as the circumcision of infants (when they were too young to understand it) was a sign and seal of God's grace under the old covenant, so baptism is a sign and seal of His grace under the new covenant. The New Testament never teaches that young children are outside God's covenant and does not classify them as "unbelievers."

It is God's grace that saves us, and God's grace always comes before our own decision. Long before a child can understand or believe—yes, even before the child exists—God initiated that child's salvation. But this is true of adults also. And in a sense, all baptisms are really "infant baptisms" (Mark 10:15; Luke 18:17). No one comes to baptism complete. It is only a beginning—in adults as well as children. So baptism celebrates prevenient grace—"the grace that comes before." No one is ever "old enough" or "knowledgeable enough" to understand the mystery of salvation. We're saved by divine grace, not by human understanding.

To ask if baptism does the baby any good is to ask the wrong question. The right question is "How is the Church proclaiming the gospel?" Baptism is not primarily an act of the parent or of the child, but of the Church, and of Christ in the Church. The Church contradicts herself when she preaches the gospel of grace and then withholds baptism from her own children. Infant baptism is the visible proclamation of the gospel.

As the Bible sees it, baptism is not primarily a sign of repentance and faith on the part of the baptized. It is not primarily our human testimony. It is rather God's covenant sign and therefore a sign of the work of God on our behalf, which precedes and makes possible our own response.

When infants are baptized, it is right and necessary that when they come to maturity they make their own confession, which involves personal repentance and faith. But they do so with the clear witness that they are saved by the work of God done for them long before they ever believed. They may possibly fail to make such confession. But this cannot be avoided by denying them baptism.

It becomes, then, the responsibility of parents, pastor, and congregation to nurture their baptized children, to teach them and guide them toward that eventual confession of personal faith.

See also
   Sacraments
   Baptism

EUCHARIST

The sacrament often called "the Lord's Supper" also goes by various other names in the New Testament and in the Christian tradition, such as "Communion," "Holy Communion," "the Supper," "the Meal," "the table of the Lord," and the "breaking of bread." One of the oldest names, and one used increasingly today, is the name "Eucharist."

"Eucharist" means "thanksgiving" and is from the Greek *eucharistein*, "to be thankful." A form of the word is found in each of the four accounts of the Last Supper (Matt. 26:26-30; Mark 14:22-26; Luke 22:14-23; 1 Cor. 11:23-26), in which Jesus gave thanks over the bread and the cup before giving them to the disciples.

In New Testament times the Lord's Supper was an occasion of joyful celebration. This was the case whenever Christians ate together, not only in the Eucharist itself, but at other times of fellowship with one another. "They broke bread in their homes and ate together with glad and sincere hearts, praising God and enjoying the favor of all the people" (Acts 2:46-47).

In the early centuries, the Eucharist was not a solemn, mournful occasion, but a festive one. By the time of the late Middle Ages, the mournful note had become the dominant one, and unfortunately this note has persisted far too long in many churches, although happily it is rapidly disappearing in much church life today. The Lord's Supper is a *feast*. It represents *fiesta*, not *funeral*.

The Church in the New Testament followed the example of Jesus in giving thanks by the use of bread and wine, probably following a Jewish pattern of praise, thanksgiving, and supplication. To its own detriment, the Church has sometimes forgotten the influence of Jewish worship on Christian eucharistic thought and practice. When this has occurred, Christian worship has tended to become weak and sentimental, losing its robustness. Just as the Jews celebrated God's mighty redemptive acts in their various festivals, so in the Eucharist Christians proclaim and celebrate the work of God in His acts of redemption.

We learn from the writings of the apostolic fathers that the New Testament note of thanksgiving continued to be sounded in connection with the Eucharist in post-New Testament times. In the epistle of Ignatius to the Ephesians is this admonition:

Gather together more frequently to celebrate God's Eucharist and to praise him. For when you meet with frequency, Satan's powers are overthrown and his destructiveness is undone by the unanimity of your faith.

The Eucharist, then, is a time for celebration, for praise, and for thanksgiving to God for His works in creation and in redemption. In the Eucharist, the Church speaks on behalf of the whole creation, for the world that God has created is represented at every Supper—in the bread and the fruit of the vine, products of the earth and of human labor; and in the people of the faithful, who make intercession for all humanity. The Eucharist thus signifies what God desires the whole world to become—an offering of praise to God the Creator, a universal communion in the Body of Christ, and a kingdom of justice, love, and peace in the Holy Spirit.

Eucharist means thanksgiving for all that God has accomplished in the *history* of salvation, for what He is doing *now* in the world and in the Church, and for the *future* fulfillment of God's kingdom, which we anticipate each time we gather at the Lord's table. When we approach the table, then, let us sing, with Charles Wesley,

> *Come, let us join with one accord*
> *Who share the supper of the Lord,*
> > *Our Lord and Master's praise to sing;*
> *Nourish'd on earth with living bread,*
> *We now are at His table fed,*
> > *But wait to see our heavenly King.*
> *To see the great Invisible*
> *Without a sacramental veil,*
> > *With all His robes of glory on,*
> *In rapturous joy and love and praise*
> *Him to behold with open face,*
> > *High on His everlasting throne.*

See also
Sacraments

PLAY

It may seem strange to think of play as one of the "words of faith," but during the 1970s a novel theological approach came on the scene known as "play theology." It soon proved itself to be a passing theological fad. But even short-lived fads sometimes make a lasting contribution, however slight, to theological understanding. Play theology made one point that is worth preserving. It is not our purpose here to explore this theme in any depth, but the point may be useful for sharpening our understanding of worship, even though it is not a particular concern of play theology to develop a theology of worship as such.

Play theology may be distinguished from "a theology of play." The latter is an attempt to offer guidelines to Christians in the use of their leisure time, to acknowledge play as necessary for a well-rounded life, and to give what might be called a "religious interpretation of play." Play theology, on the other hand, sought to give a "playful interpretation of religion." It interpreted the Christian faith in the light of the phenomenon of play.

In spite of the faddish nature of play theology, its relevance for North American religion lies in the fact that play is an important aspect of the culture at large. The spectacle of Super Bowls, World Series, and U.S. Opens, the insatiable appetite for professional and amateur sports, the thirst for entertainment, the enormous salaries paid to movie stars, rock musicians, and athletes all testify to the fact that we're a play-loving and play-worshiping society. This fact, deplorable as it may be from the standpoint of what it says about our cultural value systems, provides models, paradigms, and metaphors even for the "work" areas of life. Financiers "play the stock market," politicians devise "game plans," and military leaders engage in "war games." Play is an activity that can be found in every sector of human culture and at every stage of an individual's life.

On reflection, we can see that this universal experience bears some similarity to *religious* experience. Play is a voluntary and exhilarating activity that is separated in time, space, logic, and value from other activities. In playing we step out of our everyday workaday world and into another. But it is a world that demands serious effort and often delivers unfettered joy. Play is thus a form of transcendence that all human beings can and do experience in the everyday world of ordinary life. As such, play closely resembles religious forms of transcendence at virtually all of these points.

Thus, play offers a metaphor of faith, especially as faith expresses itself in worship. Worship is like play in that by participating in it we experience transcendence. We draw apart from the ordinary workaday world in which the greater portion of our lives is spent and transcend it by entering into the exhilaration of the holy. At least this is the way it's supposed to be.

But in many public worship services, especially in nonliturgical churches, it's easy to simply become spectators. When we "act out" our faith in singing, sacraments, and other liturgical actions, we become participants in the "game," not mere spectators in the stands. Of course, worship, like play, demands effort (if we're to benefit from it), but it can deliver unspeakable joy. For many people in society at large, play is a way to transcend the humdrum tedium and monotonous existence in which they find themselves trapped. Likewise worship, when understood as play, provides a way for the believer to transcend the ordinariness into which religious expression may too easily drift.

But this experience of transcending the tedium of daily life must not be understood as *escape*. Actually, worship is an experience of the transcendence and mystery of God precisely by virtue of the fact that it brings the holy into our mundane lives, through ordinary concrete symbols.

Take the sacraments, for example. Through the use of the common life-essential elements of water and bread, and the juice, which symbolizes blood, we are assured of God's presence in our everyday existence. Thus in the very encounter with divine transcendence through the sacraments, understood as play, we come to experience the mysterious *immanence* of the God who is Immanuel, God with us. The transcendence we experience is not escape; it is the "real presence" of God in our lives.

See also

Sacraments
Worship
Liturgy

VOCATION

I once read the testimony of a Christian businessman who said, "I own a shoe store, but my real business is outside the store, being a witness for Jesus Christ wherever I go." It made me wonder what kind of witnessing he did *inside* the store—not merely in talking to customers about Jesus, but in making sure they got good merchandise for a fair price. It seemed to me he had compartmentalized his life into two segments, one secular and one sacred.

Several years ago there was a British-produced public television series called *Upstairs, Downstairs*. It depicted life in the older mansions owned by the gentility of an earlier age. The living area, dining room, library, and drawing room were "upstairs," and the servants' quarters, basement, kitchen, and cellar were "downstairs." Those who lived upstairs were obviously higher on the social and economic scale than those who worked downstairs.

This contrast gives us a rough analogy of the differing conceptions of the religious life as held by medieval Catholicism and by the Protestant Reformation. The former made a distinction between the "sacred" (the "upstairs") and the "secular" (the "downstairs"). The highest ideal of the sacred life was to become a monk, shutting out the world, giving oneself to prayer and meditation. This was the pure "religious" calling, more pleasing to God than any "secular" alternative.

But not everyone had the temperament for this, so there was a second way for one to be a Christian. This was to remain in the secular sphere in some "worldly" occupation. Those who did not have the fortitude for the "upstairs" life could live an acceptable life "downstairs" as a butcher, baker, or candlestick maker. Those in such secular callings depended, to some extent, on the "religious" folks "upstairs" to pray them into heaven.

In the 16th century, the Protestant Reformation sought to erase such a distinction. Luther contended that the shoemaker working at his cobbler's bench was doing the work of God as surely as the priest serving Communion at the altar. The Reformers declared that there is one common level—the ground level—at which we receive the redeeming grace of God. God is no respecter of people (Rom. 2:11). The monk in the monastery or the nun in the convent has no spiritual advantage over the believing peasant working the soil or the pious mother ministering in the home. It is the New Testament message that we must overcome the world not by escaping from it, but precisely by living *in* the world where divine providence has placed us.

When Paul admonished Christians to "lead a life worthy of the calling to which you have been called" (Eph. 4:1, NRSV), he was not speaking primarily of tent making, fish mongering, or cloth weaving. He was speaking of a lifestyle that must characterize the Christian in all he or she does.

It is unfortunate that the word "vocation," or calling, has come to refer merely to the way one earns a living, what he or she does when not on *vacation*. Originally it meant the calling of a Christian *to be a Christian*, from which there is no vacation. Today if one is asked, "What is your vocation?" the likely reply will be: doctor, nurse, farmer, lawyer, teacher, to name a few examples. One might not immediately think to say, "I'm a witness for Christ." Yet, for Christians who take their primary vocation seriously, that is precisely the correct answer.

It is true that the world of the 21st century is far more complex than the world of Luther. In the interrelatedness of our technological age, with its global economy, it may be difficult to discern if we're serving God through our work—at least more difficult than it was for Luther and the shoemaker at his cobbler's bench. Some occupations today would be hard to qualify as God's work.

But if what we do for a living contributes to the betterment of humanity, rather than to its detriment, and if we give an honest day's work for the wages we earn, or sell a product at a fair price, and refuse to take advantage of anyone, then we can be sure that our "secular" work is a "sacred" Christian witness. Of course, we're supposed to witness with the mouth also, but our words count for naught if they're undercut by our work.

See also
  Laity

LAITY

I t is always regrettable when someone who is not a member of the clergy says, "I'm only a layperson," as if somehow that fact diminishes the importance of his or her role in the work of Christ's Church.

There is no word in the New Testament meaning "clergy" in the sense the word generally has meaning today. Such usage developed later. Its nearest equivalent is the Greek word *kleros*, which originally meant "lot" or "chosen by lot." It did not mean church members who were in a special class. It meant *everybody!* And the New Testament word *laos* ("laypeople") did not mean church members who were nonclergy. It meant *everybody!* Both words were used during the early centuries to describe the same people, the whole people of God. All Christians were both *laos* and *kleros!*

The New Testament word for "ministry" (*diakonia*) points to the same conclusion. Originally the word (from which our word "deacon" is derived) referred to waiting on tables (Acts 6:2; Luke 17:8). It gradually came to mean one who serves; one who ministers to others.

Unfortunately, with the passing of the centuries, and coming to a head during the Middle Ages, "clergy" and "laity" were transformed from two different forms of the same ministry into two altogether different ministries, one superior to the other.

The Protestant Reformation sought to correct this error by recovering the New Testament emphasis on the "priesthood of *all* believers." Against the medieval Roman Catholic system that made a sharp distinction between priests and laity, Martin Luther and the other Reformers insisted that every Christian is a priest, with a calling to represent others before God. The primary meaning of the priesthood of all believers was not that each Christian was his or her *own priest*, but that every Christian was a priest *to every other person.*

Thus, the priesthood of all believers was not a declaration of individuality. Instead, it made community necessary. Christians are to pray and sacrifice for one another so that through them the high priesthood of Christ may be communicated to everyone.

So far, so good. But then Protestantism developed its own distinction. It was not a distinction *between* priests and other Christians, but a distinction *within* "the priesthood of all believers"—a distinction between the "clergy" (those set apart for the service of God) and "laity" (ordinary church members).

This way of making the distinction must be called into question. Here is where Protestants are often confused and where some serious differences within Protestantism emerge—over the proper way to distinguish between "clergy" and "laity."

Of course, the Reformers understood that within the priesthood of all believers there are still "varieties of gifts" along with "the same Spirit." Therefore they set apart certain members of the Church (as the New Testament Church did, and as we still do) who were qualified by gifts, calling, and training to carry on a specialized form of ministry, often called "the ministry of Word and sacrament." This remains a necessary distinction. If everybody preached and administered the sacraments whenever he or she pleased, the result would be chaos. But the ministry of the Word and sacrament is not a "higher" ministry than that of the laity. It is simply another form of the Church's total ministry.

The Church does not *have* a ministry. The Church *is* ministry—the ministry of the ordained clergy and the ministry of the laity. These are not two different ministries, but two forms of the very same ministry. "Now there are varieties of gifts, but the same Spirit; and there are varieties of services, but the same Lord; and there are varieties of activities, but it is the same God who activates all of them in everyone" (1 Cor. 12:4-6, NRSV).

All believers are to be priests, "offering spiritual sacrifices acceptable to God through Jesus Christ" (1 Pet. 2:5).

So let no one say "I am *only* a layperson," for there is nothing higher on earth than to be part of the people of God, the priesthood of all believers.

See also
   Vocation

NEIGHBOR

J esus said, "Love your neighbor as yourself" (Mark 12:31). This is often read as if He said, "Love your neighbor as *you love* yourself." But He didn't say that. Historic Christianity has always defined self-love as sin. What Jesus commands is that I love my neighbors as if they were my own self. Because they *are*! The Christian finds his or her identity in Christ and in his or her neighbor. "We are members of one another" (Eph. 4:25, NRSV). We find ourselves when we lose ourselves in others for Christ's sake (Matt. 10:39). This is not self-love; it is self-*giving*

For the children of this world, love is *eros*. The Greek word *eros* (the root of our word "erotic") refers to the love that is aroused by something desirable in its object. It may be the desire for sexual gratification, or it may be the quest for wisdom. It may even be the desire for God, if God is seen as desirable for the benefits He can bring.

For the children of God, love is *agape*—the love that springs out of its own source, which is God's gift of fellowship with himself. It is what the German language calls *quellende liebe*—a springing up and overflowing of love in the heart, which requires no stimulus from outside. It is the love that looks for nothing in return. Christian love, then, is love of the neighbor.

When asked "Who is my neighbor?" Jesus answered with the parable of the Good Samaritan. My neighbor is anyone whose need makes such a demand on me that I cannot in good conscience turn aside as did the priest and the Levite. Those two lost something of themselves that day by turning aside from their neighbor. But the Samaritan expressed what he had already found—he had value as he valued others.

The neighbor is God's *representative* in this present evil world, appointed by God to receive the sacrifices of love and service, which God does not require to be given to himself directly. The Christian offers his or her gift of love and service to God through his or her neighbor. The divine love (*agape*) comes down from eternity in a U-shaped curve: God loves us, and we in turn are to pass that love on to our neighbor. In that way, God's love comes back to Him again. The Christian is a channel, open upward to heaven by faith and outward to his or her neighbor through love. All that the Christian possesses has been received from God that it may be passed on. We have nothing of our own to give; we are but instruments through which redeeming love is further mediated. Thus, the Christian is called to be a "Christ" to his or her neighbor.

Our neighbor represents the *invisible* Christ. What we do to our neighbor we do not only in this present world, but in the eternal world as well. Our Lord taught that the good that we do to one of the least of Christ's brothers, we do to Him (Matt. 25:40).

The neighbor also represents the *risen* Christ. Christ has been triumphant over Satan and the powers of darkness. But Satan is still permitted to go about this world like a roaring lion, seeking whom he may devour. Our faith and our worship must therefore express Christ's final victory here and now. Our life together in the Spirit must have the joy that is the foretaste of the final victory of the redeemed in heaven.

It is in the context of the ascended glory of the risen Christ that the biblical idea of the neighbor is to be understood. God has promised that we "may participate in the divine nature" (2 Pet. 1:4). "To become divine" was a phrase common in the earlier Christian centuries. But its meaning varied. To Catholics in both the East and the West, it meant to become immortal, or to become one endued with supernatural powers. To mystics it meant to become one with the Infinite. For the monk of the Middle Ages it meant to become master of the passions and therefore of nature itself.

All those meanings are at best only partially true. Martin Luther was closer to our Lord's meaning. He said, "We become divine through love, which causes us to do good to our neighbor, for divine nature is nought else than the sheer doing of good" (*The Works of Martin Luther*, X, 1, 100).

"To become divine through love!" That is why we need our neighbor. Even more than our neighbor needs us!

See also
Laity
Vocation

KINGDOM

T he concept of the kingdom, or reign, of God was the central theme of the teaching of Jesus.

With this theme Jesus began His preaching ministry. "'The time has come,' he said. 'The kingdom of God is near. Repent and believe the good news!'" (Mark 1:15). The Kingdom is a major theme in the sayings and parables of Jesus, and it is a theme on His lips at the Last Supper.

It should be noted that the Gospels use two phrases, "the Kingdom of heaven" and "the Kingdom of God." Their meanings are identical. Matthew prefers the former phrase, doubtless because he, more than the other Gospel writers, is writing for a Jewish readership. The name of God was so sacred that no devout Jew would utter it lightly. One way to avoid doing so was to speak of heaven instead, and so instead of writing about "the kingdom of God," he speaks of "the kingdom of heaven." In contrast, Mark and Luke use "the kingdom of God" exclusively.

It should also be noted that the word "kingdom" in modern speech denotes a territory, an area of land. But this is not its meaning in the New Testament. There it refers to the sovereignty of God, a state or condition of things in which God rules and reigns supreme. Paul tells us that the kingdom of God is "righteousness, peace and joy in the Holy Spirit" (Rom. 14:17).

As the New Testament writers seek to interpret the meaning of the concept, they understand the kingdom of God in three tenses—past, present, and future.

The Kingdom is a *past* reality; God has established His reign on earth through the life, death, and resurrection of Jesus. To do so was His purpose in the history of Israel and, before that, in the very creation of the world itself. The reign of God was manifest in the deeds of Jesus, and this means principally in His miracles. For instance, His casting-out of demons could mean only that an assault was being made upon the kingdom of evil. Such miracles are enacted proclamations that the kingdom of God has come.

The Kingdom is a *present* reality; God continues His activity of

Kingdom-building through the work of the Holy Spirit in the Church. Some of the Lord's sayings and parables speak of the coming of the kingdom of God in the *present*. God's rule is therefore now within the grasp of all who will reach out and receive it.

Some of our Lord's sayings and parables speak of the *future* coming of the Kingdom. Jesus taught us to pray for the coming of this future reality (Matt. 6:10). As we pray for the coming of God's kingdom, we do so in the midst of a world and in the midst of a history where evil seems never to subside. We nevertheless believe in the promise of ultimate victory. We know we already have "redemption through his blood, the forgiveness of sins" (Eph. 1:7). We believe in the promise of our resurrection from the dead, and we live in hope for the fulfillment of this promise. We believe in, and hope for, Christ's second coming—the triumphant worldwide manifestation of Christ's presence. We believe in and hope for an everlasting reign of universal peace and the final total defeat of all the evil powers. We believe in the final judgment and in the separation of those who resolutely and finally refuse the offer of salvation. We believe in the promise of glorification, a prospect that is totally indescribable from our present perspective but for which we wait and hope with glad expectation.

And we believe the end of this earthly order will come, but such an end will be the *telos*, the goal, of creation and the fulfillment of history. This is why it is sometimes called "the final cosummation." We do not believe that the world will totally cease to exist but that "this world in its present form" will pass away (1 Cor. 7:31), and all that is good about this present existence will be incorporated into a new heaven and a new earth. This new cosmos will be free of all conflict, when Christ "hands over the kingdom to God the Father after he has destroyed all dominion, authority and power" (1 Cor. 15:24). And thus we pray the prayer our Lord taught us to pray: "Thy kingdom come." And we pray the prayer with which the Bible ends: "Come, Lord Jesus" (Rev. 22:20).

See also
   Millennium
   Church

PAROUSIA

The Greek word *parousia* means "arrival" or "presence." In the ancient world the word referred to the visit of a king to one of his provinces. The term is used in Christian theology to designate the second coming of Christ. Although the term "second coming" itself is not found in Scripture, the idea behind the phrase is a prominent New Testament theme.

Scripture does not tell us the *time* of the *parousia*. Both Matthew (24:36) and Mark (13:32) declare that the hour is known to no one, not even to the Son of Man himself, but only to the Father. Elsewhere we are warned that He will come unannounced, as a thief in the night (1 Thess. 5:2; Rev. 3:3; 16:15). And yet the Gospels describe signs of His coming that should be sufficient to alert the watchful.

The images used in the New Testament to describe the *parousia* are derived in part from Dan. 7:13-14, according to which the coming of the Son of Man will bring about the defeat of all evil powers and establish an everlasting and indestructible kingdom.

In its teaching about what we call "the Second Coming," the New Testament places the emphasis not on "second" but on "coming." To do otherwise would suggest that Christ was present once, then was gone, and then will be present once again. Some passages may seem to describe such a situation. But we must balance this with promises such as "I am with you always, to the very end of the age" (Matt. 28:20). We must conclude that the *parousia* is a coming of one who is already present—a unique and complete manifestation of a presence whom we now see only partially and glimpse through a glass darkly.

The *parousia* is not the return of a Christ who has been absent from the world since the Ascension. It would even be improper to say that it is the *bodily* return of one who has been absent *in body*, because the New Testament describes the Church as His Body, and through the Church Christ has been "bodily" present in the world throughout the intervening centuries. Furthermore, we partake of

Christ's "body" each time we gather at the Lord's table and receive the bread of the Eucharist. He is not absent from the table; His "real presence" is there.

The *parousia* will be the completion of that which was begun in Christ's resurrection. It is the final stage of God's coming to the world in a history that finds its center in Jesus Christ. From the perspective of Christology, it is the universal manifestation of Christ's Lordship. From the perspective of Creation, it is the world's arrival at its destiny. The Second Coming is not the return of a Lord who has been absent, but the complete and victorious breaking through of a presence that has been hitherto partially hidden by the veil of sin and evil. The resurrected mode of Christ's existence will in this event be so thoroughly actualized in the world that it can no longer be hidden.

Since the *parousia* is ultimately the free act of God, and since God has revealed little explicit information concerning its temporal or spatial details, we are largely dependent upon the Bible's language of images and metaphors. Much of this imagery is cast in the language of worship, especially in the note of anticipation that is sounded in the Eucharist, which we are to observe "until he comes" (1 Cor. 11:26). The Lord's Supper is but the foretaste of the final Kingdom, an "appetizer" for the heavenly banquet in which "people will come from east and west and north and south, and will take their places at the feast in the kingdom of God" (Luke 13:29). The *parousia* is the highest realization of that which even now takes place when we celebrate the Eucharist: God's communion with His people.

The Christ of the *parousia* will be none other than the Christ who was incarnate, crucified, and raised, and who has remained present in His Church through the Holy Spirit. The new element will be its worldwide scope and its indescribable glory. In trying to describe it now, we can only stammer in verbal images, but in faith we confess that in His second coming Christ will be visible over the whole world as the center of a redeemed humanity of which He is the Creator.

————

See also
   Advent

ADVENT

A dvent is the season of the Christian year when the Church turns its gaze in two directions—past and future. It looks backward as it prepares to celebrate the birth of Christ in Bethlehem, and it looks forward as it engages in self-examination in preparation for Christ's second coming in glory to judge the living and the dead.

The word "advent" comes from the Latin *adventus*, which means "coming" or "arrival." Thus, in certain contexts its meaning is the same as the Greek *parousia*, treated elsewhere in this book. However, the latter term occurs in the New Testament only with reference to the *Second* Coming. During the Advent season, both "comings" of Christ are embraced in the Church's worship—His coming in the Incarnation and His coming at the end of the age. Some Advent hymns blend the joy of the Good News of Christ's nativity with the expectation of the Second Coming.

Christian prayer during Advent might be summed up in one word: "Come." It is the "Come, Lord Jesus,' with which the Book of Revelation ends. Although Christ has been present in the world all along (Matt. 28:20), we pray for His presence to take on a special intensity during Advent.

Advent always includes the four Sundays preceding Christmas. The commercialism that marks this time of year would lead us to think that the main focus of the season is the spreading of Christmas cheer through the buying and giving of gifts. But Advent is primarily concerned with preparing for Christ's second coming in the light of the hope made clear to us by His first coming.

Advent is a season of tension and paradox. In the Church's calendar, the first Sunday of Advent is called the beginning of the Christian year. Yet it plunges us headlong into the tension between the "already" of Christ's coming in the flesh and the "not yet" of the consummation of all things in Christ at the end of the age. Interestingly, we begin the Christian year reflecting on the end of all human history.

Advent is the time of thanksgiving for God's "unspeakable gift" of Christ, which has already taken place, and a time of anticipation of the Second Coming for which we pray and hope. We rejoice in the angels' song of "peace on earth" and the "good news of great joy" that they announced to the shepherds; and we also pray, "Thy kingdom come. Thy will be done in earth, as it is in heaven" (Matt. 6:10, KJV).

The prophetic note is especially strong during these days of Advent. We pray for the destruction of all evil powers, for the triumph of the righteousness and justice of God, and for the dawning of God's peace over all the nations. This glorious prospect was illuminated by Christ's first coming at Bethlehem where "the hopes and fears of all the years" were met on that holy night. Thus, our worship, praying, singing, and celebration of the gospel during these weeks should joyfully focus on the Christian hope for the future.

This sheds light on our Christmas celebrations. Christmas is far richer and deeper than a mere sentimental remembrance of the birth of Jesus. Of course, we should value the intimacy and tenderness of the image of the "sweet little Jesus boy, born in a manger," but Christmas means much more. "Joy to the world! the Lord is come!" is a reminder that the One who came to Bethlehem is indeed our Redeemer—the One into whose dying and rising we are baptized (Rom. 6:4), just as He was baptized in the Jordan and into our human condition. When we understand Christmas this way, our worship will speak to our deepest needs and connect with our most profound experiences.

God's advent among us is so profound that we can never fully grasp the mystery of incarnate deity. So we must continue to remember and experience anew, year after year, the reality of light in the midst of the world's darkness. At Advent we experience the fear, joy, and hope that Christian worship expresses in the story of God's coming to judge the world in the form of a helpless Child lying in a manger made of wood that foreshadows the wooden Cross on which He gave His life to "save His people from their sins."

See also
   Parousia

TIME

What is time? It has become customary in theology to differentiate between two concepts of time, one *cyclical*, the other *linear*. According to most theologians, the biblical understanding of time is linear and thus different from the cyclical understanding that predominated in nonbiblical religions.

Of course, we all experience time as linear. That is, everyone knows that time passes away, that the present moment is soon gone, never to return. The movement from the "not yet" to the "now" and onward to the "no longer" is irreversible. Time is a one-way street; we experience it in a straight line.

But time as *experienced* is different from time as *understood*. Adherents of nonbiblical religions understood time as part and parcel of nature, as something integral to the ever-revolving natural processes that have neither beginning nor end. They conceived time as circular. The experience of time was part of an eternal process. Individuals are mortal and transient, but the forces of nature are eternal and unchanging. Thus, mortal human beings, by seeing themselves as an integral part of nature, could believe that they shared somehow in the eternity of nature. Life was understood as forever moving through the inevitable cycle of seedtime and harvest, birth and rebirth, life and death.

According to this cyclical view of history, that which is true is timeless. What really matters is eternity, and eternity is timelessness. Time as we know it in human history is just a shadow of the eternal, or a dirty mirror that occasionally reflects eternal principles. Thus, the future could not be important because it could not bring anything that was essentially new. This view, understood by primitive peoples and later refined in Greek philosophy, became an integral part of the Western history of ideas.

By contrast, most scholars agree that the Judeo-Christian tradition sees time as linear. The symbol is a straight line, not a circle. Time has a beginning. God's creation of the world was the creation of time, for time as we know it is determined by the earth's rotation and its revolution around the sun. Just as God stands above the world, although immanent within it, He also stands above time, although immanent within it.

Just as time has a beginning, it will have an end. It will be gathered up and fulfilled in eternity. It is only by the clear delineation of time as having a beginning and an end that the cyclical view of time is overthrown and the straight line and not the circle becomes its proper symbol. The beginning and the end are held together by God's eternal plan, and God manifests His Lordship over time by the fact that from the beginning He aims at the end.

To speak of eternity, therefore, is to speak of God, who is Lord of time just as He is Lord of the world. Eternity is neither "endless time" nor "the negation of time." God has created it just as He has created the world, and He wills that time, like the world, will be filled with His glory. He wills that the end of time will be the consummation of time that is filled with eternity.

Christian faith holds that Jesus Christ is the center of history. As the center, He holds together the beginning of time and the end of time. The apostle Paul in two majestic passages (Eph. 1:7-23 and Col. 1:13-23) proclaims that Christ is both the ground and the goal of creation; He is both the world's whence and its whither: "All things were created by him and for him" (Col. 1:16). It is striking that the apostle's bold assertions that the entire cosmos holds together in Christ occur in the midst of his confession of faith in the Atonement. In Christ we have "redemption through his blood, the forgiveness of sins" (Eph. 1:7; see also Col. 1:14).

Three realities are thus bound together—the Creation, the Atonement, and the Consummation. The reason is obvious—sin blurs our vision until we can see neither our own personal ground nor the ground of the cosmos; neither our own personal destiny nor the destiny of the cosmos. Only in Jesus Christ and the atonement He made for sin, and the forgiveness that issues from it, do we apprehend the whence (the ground of creation) as identical with the whither (the goal of creation). Time is thus understood in the light of the end for which it was created, and this can be no other than the goal of human history—Christ the hope of glory.

See also
   Death

DEATH

C hristian faith takes death seriously. Death is real; it is not an illusion that can be banished by wishful thinking. It is one thing that all human beings have in common. In spite of modern advances in medical science, 100 percent of all human beings die! It does not finally matter that we may reduce the number of people who die from cancer or heart disease, or that we prolong life so that the average age of people grows steadily greater. When all the figures are totaled up, they will show that the human mortality rate remains at a constant 100 percent. We must not be lulled into a false security that fails to take death in utter seriousness.

Death is therefore the first word that must be said about human existence. From the moment we are born, we march inexorably toward our death. This fact gives urgency to life and to time. Our time on earth has an end. Time is not an endless cyclical repetition of moments. If time were endless, it could not be wasted. It is only because we do not have an inexhaustible supply of time that we can speak about wasting time. Therefore, what happens while time lasts is of supreme importance.

Although death is the first word to be said about human existence, it is not the *last* word. Because death is not the end, the life that ends in death takes on ultimate significance. "It is appointed for mortals to die once, and after that the judgment" (Heb. 9:27, NRSV). Between those two events—death and judgment—lies the resurrection of the dead (John 5:28-29; Acts 24:15).

Most of the world's religions base their hope for life after death on the idea of the "immortality of the soul,' which is the belief that there is an essential part of the self that death cannot destroy. This idea was held by the Greek philosophers, such as Socrates and Plato. Under the influence of such philosophy, many Christians have also believed in immortality, but it is not the category used in the New Testament to describe life after death. In the Apostles' Creed we do not confess faith in the "immortality of the soul, and the life everlasting," but rather in "the resurrection of the body, and the life everlasting." All the great creeds of Christendom likewise affirm the same truth. Belief in the immortality of the soul rests its hope for life after death on what we are by nature, whereas Christian faith rests it on what God does for us by grace. It is not creation but *redemption* that gives us hope.

Against the human-centered concept of immortality, Christian faith, in holding to the biblical teaching of "the resurrection of the body," grounds the hope of eternal life in God's gracious promise of redemption rather than in some part, aspect, or quality that humanity has by nature. The doctrine of resurrection takes death seriously. Something that has not died cannot be raised from the dead! In the Greek view of immortality, the body is only a prison of the soul. The soul is the real person; the body is merely a disposable appendage, a hindrance to the soul's freedom and enjoyment. The soul is created immortal; therefore, that which is the real person cannot die. In such a dualistic view, death is taken lightly. Death is a friend; it is that which allows us to escape this imprisoning body.

But nowhere in the Bible is the human soul regarded as naturally immortal. The only way in which human beings can live again after death is by a resurrection—by a miracle. One can see the difference in the two views by comparing the ways Socrates and Jesus approached their deaths. Socrates drank the hemlock gladly, because he believed death was a blessed escape from the prison of the body. But Jesus sweat great drops of blood in Gethsemane when He knew that death was near. In Christian faith death is never a friend—it is an enemy. But Christ met the enemy head-on and defeated it by His own death and resurrection. Therefore, believers do not have to fear it. Because they are redeemed, they can rejoice with the apostle Paul because "death has been swallowed up in victory—

Where, O death, is your victory?
Where, O death, is your sting?" (1 Cor. 15:54-55).

See also
Resurrection
Time

JUDGMENT

Are you ready for the judgment day?" Those words of the invitation song often sung at revivals when I was a child struck fear to my heart. But the Hebrew word *shafat* ("to judge") is not so frightening. It means "to establish the right order of things." That's what God purposes to do—establish a new order in a world that is bent, an order in which evil will be defeated and righteousness will reign. It is the new order that Mary sang about in her hymn of praise, in which rulers are brought down from their thrones and the humble are lifted up (Luke 1:46-55).

Christians confess their hope for this new order, promised at the birth of Christ in Bethlehem. But because this promised work of God is not yet completed and oppression and injustice are still pervasive, Christians confess their faith in a Last Judgment in which that work will be finalized in conjunction with Christ's return at the Last Day.

The best clues to the future are to be found in history. God's action in the future will be consistent with His action in the past. There is yet little to be seen of the new order sung about in Mary's Magnificat, but faith perceives just enough of God's judging in history to take courage for the future. In God's acts in history and in the present, we can see preambles of His eventual liberating judgment, which will make straight forever this crooked and disrupted human existence.

By what criterion will we be judged? Surely the biblical witness is clear: we will be judged on the basis of our response to the love of God as revealed to us in Christ. The three parables of the Judgment in Matt. 25 describe this response. In the parable of the ten virgins, we are judged by the watchfulness and carefulness with which we make preparation in this life for the next. In the parable of the talents, the issue is how wisely we use what we have been given. And in the parable of the sheep and goats, the criterion is the degree of our compassion for our fellow human beings, even when we're not aware that we're doing God's work.

The New Testament describes judgment as both a reality in this present life (John 3:18; Rom. 1:18-32) and a reality at the last day (Rev. 20:11-15). Since the basis of judgment is our relationship to Christ, we can see the link between the present and future aspects of judgment. The final judgment will be the divine ratification of the relationship (either positive or negative) with Christ that we have chosen in this life.

But the Last Judgment will be different from the preambles of it that we see now. Judgment in this present life is not final. Here and now, people created with freedom can still change sides. The loving purpose of the present judgments of God is to bring about just such a result. Although the Bible says little about the matter, there is no biblical evidence that the final choices made in this life are reversible after death.

Perplexing questions arise. When and where does the Last Judgment take place? Will all humanity be gathered together in one place and at one time to be judged? Or does each person face judgment at death? Both images can be found in the New Testament. And that is the crucial word—"image." The Bible describes such matters in the language of imagery—pictures, portrayals, and metaphors describing the seriousness of the Final Judgment. But we are not given schedules, locations, or logistics.

Still other issues present themselves. What about people who have never heard the gospel? Or those who heard it inadequately presented? Or those mentally unable to respond to it?

Such people can surely be trusted to God, who will deal with them not arbitrarily but consistent with His nature as holy love as that love is revealed in Christ. This much we know: according to Jesus' account of the separation of the sheep and the goats (Matt. 25:31-46), the final Judgment will contain two big surprises: (1) Many who did not know it in this life will find that they have been on God's side all along, and (2) Many who thought themselves righteous will be cast out. Are you a sheep or a goat?

See also
  Death
  Resurrection
  Hell

HELL

We say little about hell these days, perhaps as a reaction against some past preachers who used the subject as a "scare tactic." Maybe it's time to revisit the theme.

In his play *No Exit*, Jean Paul Sartre, the French atheistic philosopher, has one of his characters say, "Hell is other people!"

I would say just the opposite: "Hell is to be finally and utterly *alone*." Is that biblical? Granted, there are no proof-texts that say exactly that. But it is a truth inherent in the biblical doctrine of sin. Sin is pictured in the Bible and in the historic Christian tradition as the illusion of self-rule. It is finding the meaning of life in self rather than in others and in the Other. Or it may manifest itself as the choice to place ultimate trust in the wrong "other," to let some wrong "other" make our choices for us. In either case, sin is becoming Lord over one's own life, determining for oneself what is good and what is evil (Gen. 3:5, 22).

God commanded Adam and Eve not to eat from a certain tree in the garden (Gen. 2:17). For them, that fruit would have been evil. But Eve "saw that the fruit of the tree was good" (3:6). She seized for herself the right to do the labeling.

Matt. 12:22-37 makes much the same point in reverse. The Pharisees saw a good thing (the healing of a demoniac) and called it evil. They changed the labels. To do that is to blaspheme the Holy Spirit, which Jesus calls the unpardonable sin! It is not that God will not pardon. But people who persistently desire nothing more than their own way, as opposed to God's will, and insist on defining good and evil for themselves have slammed the door in the face of forgiveness.

Thus, the biblical understanding of sin gives us insight into the meaning of hell. God never sends people to hell; hell is what we choose for ourselves. God did not even create hell for human beings; it was made "for the devil and his angels" (Matt. 25:41). But God created us with freedom. When in our freedom we choose a self-centered existence, God allows us to have what we want. It is

God's respect for human freedom that makes hell possible. Hell expresses the possibility that a person can reject the love of God and thus choose isolation rather than communion. It is the ultimate expression of our own choice against God. C. S. Lewis describes the condemned as those to whom God, after much patience, finally says, "Your will be done" (*The Great Divorce*, 72).

The New Testament declares, "God is love" (1 John 4:8, 16). Since He loves everyone, He treats the actions of each person as significant. This truth is safeguarded by the idea that every person must eventually give account to God for his or her actions. True love never forces itself on its object. God's love means that we have freedom to accept or spurn that love. To reject the idea of condemnation—and of hell—would mean a rejection of freedom.

Hell is not God's punishment for choosing the wrong road; it is simply where the road leads. Hell is the Father's heartbroken willingness to give His prodigal children what they so relentlessly demand; it is a teardrop on the cheek of grace and a sigh on the lips of mercy.

Hell is the expression not of God's anger, but of His agony, an agony that says, "I will give you what you want; in life you wanted your own way, you lived only for self, you wanted nothing but self—now take it." It would not be erroneous to say, "If I go to hell, I'll be the only one there." For hell is utter self-chosen aloneness.

Traditional images of hell as a place of "fire and brimstone" where the cries of the damned are heard continuously, may have value in picturing such a horrible fate. But the most significant thing about the destiny of the finally impenitent is not the temperature nor the acoustics. Final destiny will be decided on the basis of one's relationship to the God who is love. The truly horrible thing will be that the impenitent, of their own free choice, will have cut themselves off from God, from God's people, and from God's good creation. Could a worse hell be imagined?

See also
    Sin
    Judgment

MILLENNIUM

M illennium" comes from the Latin numerical word meaning "one thousand." Millennialism is the view, held by many evangelical Christians, that Christ will return to earth and set up a visible kingdom that will last 1,000 years. Mention of a millennium is found in only one biblical passage: Rev. 20:1-6.

Three major theories address how this thousand-year reign relates chronologically to the Second Coming: premillennialism (the Second Coming will precede the thousand-year reign of Christ), postmillennialism (the Second Coming will follow the thousand-year reign), and amillennialism (there will be no literal, earthly, thousand-year reign). In each theory are variations and subtheories.

Creating further complexity are the debates concerning the time of the event mentioned in Scripture as the Great Tribulation. Then there is the question of the "Rapture," which premillennialists usually distinguish from the Second Coming itself, which supposedly comes later. A subdivision of premillennialism is dispensationalism, with its speculative charts and timetables. Confusion galore!

We know that the Book of Revelation belongs to that genre of literature called "apocalyptic," which is characterized by many symbols and images (candlesticks, angels, strange beasts, numbers, geometric figures, harlots, lambs, lions, and stars). Such images are generally understood in a symbolic or metaphorical sense. That is, they are not taken literally but point to something rich and meaningful. Oddly, most millennialists tend to take literally the thousand years in Rev. 20:1-6, even though they may inconsistently admit to the symbolic nature of almost everything else in Revelation!

How, then, are we to understand the "thousand years"? The answer seems simple—almost too simple! To our shame, we theologians are sometimes guilty of "turning wine into water" by taking the simple but sparkling truths of the gospel and transforming them into ideas that are complex but bland and unexciting.

The writer of Revelation apparently did not have at hand a numerical concept higher than 1,000. It was a great number for the people of that time. They could not have understood the size of the universe in which the distance between galaxies must be measured in "light-years." A thousand was a superlative. Even when the truth the writer wished to express called for a much greater number, he still was forced to write in terms of "thousands," as when he described the angelic chorus as "numbering thousands upon thousands, and ten thousand times ten thousand" (Rev. 5:11).

So what may the writer of Revelation mean by the millennium? Maybe simply this: our future in Christ, which words cannot adequately describe, will be the most glorious thing we have ever experienced. It will be superlative! To describe the future of God's faithful people as a thousand years in which they will reign with Christ is to say, "It will be magnificent, and it will be forever!"

Granted, there are chronological elements in the millennium passage. But can we not see in the binding of Satan for a "thousand years" an affirmation of the enemy's total defeat? So why is he described as being loosed again after the thousand years and allowed to wreak havoc awhile longer? Perhaps to drive home the point that no matter how much leeway Satan is given (note the Book of Job) God is ruler yet, and Christ is Conqueror of every foe! This is certainly the message the writer of the book would know that his intended readers near the dawn of the second century would need to hear in the midst of the persecutions they were to endure.

To those readers, the greatest encouragement would come from an understanding that such a "millennial" victory was not solely something awaiting them out in the far distant future. They would need to be encouraged in the present. Thus, in the picture of the millennium, we can see a "realized" element. To live this present life in the power of the Holy Spirit is to live the life of eternity, the life of the Kingdom. The millennium, therefore, is both "already" and "not yet."

Then are we living in the "last days"? Yes! And we have been since Christ was raised from the dead!

See also
   Kingdom

GLORIFICATION

I n Scripture the words "glory" and "glorification" are rich in meaning. In the Old Testament, "glory" belonged to God alone. When Moses prayed to be shown God's glory, God hid him in a cleft of a rock so that he could not see God's face (Exod. 33:18-23). But the New Testament proclaims that the glory of God has been revealed to us in Jesus Christ (2 Cor. 4:6), and that through the Spirit we may reflect that same glory (2 Cor. 3:18).

Glorification has a future aspect also. It is that which we confess in the words of the Apostles' Creed: "I believe in . . . the resurrection of the body, and the life everlasting. Amen." This sums up our hope for the future.

But we could not so confidently confess this hope were it not based on realities in the history of salvation and in our own personal history. The "life everlasting" has come already in the Christ who gave His life for the sake of the kingdom of God. Because of His utter self-sacrifice, God raised Him from the dead. And this life has come to all who have been "buried with him through baptism" and raised to a new life (Rom. 6:4), having believed in Him as "the resurrection and the life" (John 11:25). In the writings of John, eternal life is almost completely seen as a life here and now—"eternal life begun below," as an old Gospel song expresses it.

Yet it must be said that all these present gifts point us toward the future. "If only for this life we have hope in Christ, we are to be pitied more than all men" (1 Cor. 15:19). Concerning the future life, glorification stands for our participation in a renewed form of human existence that has been made known to us in the risen Christ.

Among the persistent aspirations of the human race is the vision of a time of peace and blessedness when the suffering and agony of human history will be overcome.

In the language of worship and piety, the most common term for this expectation is "heaven." Heaven is beyond our human ability to fully comprehend. At the least, it will be the final, fulfilling relationship between God and His creation that has been realized in Christ and remains to be realized in the rest of humanity. Heaven is that which Jesus went to prepare for us when He returned to the Father (John 14:3). Heaven, then, is the consequence of His resurrection and ascension.

The "life everlasting" has been described in different ways in the biblical and historical traditions. Many Catholics have longed for the "beatific vision" of seeing God face-to-face. The Epistle to the Hebrews speaks of a "rest" for God's people, a meaningful metaphor for people who struggle and labor in this life. But "rest" may not be everyone's aspiration. In a world where human labor is often an unfulfilling drudgery, many people long for creative tasks that are meaningful, for work that is artistic rather than drab, where, in the words of Rudyard Kipling in *L'Envoi*,

> Each for the joy of the working,
> And each, in his separate star,
> Shall draw the Thing as he sees It
> For the God of Things as they are!

And in a divided world torn by strife, where there is loneliness and alienation, a meaningful metaphor for many people today is that of "community." Concepts of beatific vision, rest, and creativity emphasize individuality. Of course, individuality is significant. Unlike the various forms of pure mysticism, Christianity looks for a future in which there is interpersonal dialogue and relationship rather than the loss of identity through being absorbed into the Absolute. But as we already see in this present life, true individuality develops only within community. The corporate dimension is the controlling one. The Bible is rich with images depicting life everlasting as an active participation with all the redeemed in a perfect fellowship, with Christ as the center.

Furthermore, to the corporate must be added the *cosmic*, for the whole creation shares in God's redemptive plan. For the completion of that divine plan we wait "in eager expectation" and "in hope that the creation itself will be liberated from its bondage to decay and brought into the glorious freedom of the children of God" (Rom. 8:19-21). "Amen. Even so, come, Lord Jesus!" (Rev. 22:20, NKJV).

See also
   Resurrection
   Kingdom

WORKS CITED

Brunner, Emil. *Dogmatics Vol. 1: The Christian Doctrine of God*. London: Lutterworth Press, 1966.

Dunning, H. Ray. *Grace, Faith, and Holiness: A Wesleyan Systematic Theology*. Kansas City: Beacon Hill Press of Kansas City, 1988.

Lewis, C. S. *The Great Divorce*. New York: Macmillan Publishing Co., 1946.

Lindsell, Harold. *The Battle for the Bible*. Grand Rapids: Zondervan Publishing House, 1976.

Lodahl, Michael. *The Story of God: Wesleyan Theology and Biblical Narrative*. Kansas City: Beacon Hill Press of Kansas City, 1994.

Luther, Martin. *The Works of Martin Luther*. Edited by Jaroslav Pelikan and Helmut T. Lehmann. Philadelphia: Mulhenberg Press, 1959.

Orwell, George. *1984*. New York: Penguin Books, 1949.

The Standard Sermons of John Wesley. Edited by E. H. Sugden. London: Epworth Press, 1931.

Temple, William. *Readings in St. John's Gospel*. London: Macmillan and Co. Ltd., 1970.

Walker, Alice. *The Color Purple*. New York: Washington Square Press, 1982.

Wesley, John. *The Letters of Rev. John Wesley*. Edited by John Telford. London: Epworth Press, 1931.

Wesley, John. *The Works of John Wesley*. Kansas City: Beacon Hill Press of Kansas City, 1978.